Breakthrough Leadership

Chip Townsend and Jody Holland

D1293498

PRAISE FOR BREAKTHROUGH LEADERSHIP

"Fantastic ! This is the Right Book, at the Right Time on the Right Topic. It is an awe inspiring read that not only teaches, informs and motivates, but refreshingly excites the reader to better themselves, even when all odds are against them.

This great "TOOL" needs to be in the hands of all leaders in all industries, and those that aspire to become one.

Your book sent me on an eye opening, soul searching mission, and after 41 years in the martial arts, I am now ready to take up the challenge to better myself like never before!

Yours in martial arts,"

SHIHAN PHIL ANDERSON
NMA / ISKA South Africa

"Turning tragedy into triumph was a personal strength Chip Townsend was forced to develop in early childhood. Now, this successful martial arts businessman and world breaking champion provides a leadership guide just as inspiring as his own personal story. Read it and reap!"

John Corcoran
Hall of Fame author/journalist
MANAGING EDITOR, "MARTIAL ARTS

SUCCESS" MAGAZINE

".... I think it is excellent. It is well written with great lessons and stories that every reader will benefit from. I especially liked the line 'It isn't having a black belt that matters. It is being a black belt that matters.' I am going to add that to my arsenal immediately.

Congratulations on a job well done."

Dave Kovar
CEO OF KOVAR SYSTEMS

"Chip Townsend has created a principle centered Masterpiece in his book Breakthrough Leadership. In it you will learn easy, actionable strategies to bring out the leader that lies within you. It is a great read for a person just starting out or as a source of timeless reminders for someone who is already in a Leadership position."

Christopher Rappold
Founder, Personal Best Karate
5 Time World Champion
Executive Director, Team Paul Mitchell

"Encouraging and equipping those of us who are devoted to teaching martial arts and rescuing us when questioning this calling from time to time. Very seldom can you digest text knowing that it comes from genuine origin with truthful intent. Of course it helps knowing the person. But then again who out there doesn't know Master Chip?"

Kancho Paul Cave
NMA/ISKA South Africa

"Over the past decade or more, I have known of the reputation of Team Chip Tae Kwon Do in our city. It is known as a place that develops discipline, excellence and integrity in the lives of its students - all attributes of Godly character. A couple of years ago I had the privilege of getting to know Chip and Glyn Ann Townsend, and I began to understand where that reputation came from. They are a man and woman who live what they teach. And now they've done each of us a tremendous service by putting the foundations of what they impart to their students into an incredible book so we can all glean from their insights. I just finished reading Breakthrough Leadership, and I can tell you - your life will be bettered through reading and implementing its wisdom.

David McQueen Senior Pastor Beltway Park Church, Abilene, TX."

DEDICATION

For Chip, the dedication is to my wife, kids, and parents. My mom and dad are celebrating 50 years of marriage today as I type, April 17, 2014. They have been hugely instrumental to my personal development.   And to Jody for encouraging this adventure!

Ephesians 2:10 (ESV) "For we are His workmanship, created in Christ Jesus, for good works which God prepared beforehand that we should walk in them."

For Jody, the dedication is to the host of marital artists that I have had the honor to know throughout my life. I have studied multiple styles, all with the common principle. I am honored to have co-authored this book with Master Chip Townsend and have been blessed by getting to know his team of incredible black belts.

CONTENTS

ACKNOWLEDGMENTS

We would like to acknowledge and thank John Corcoran for his formatting suggestions on the book. We would like to acknowledge Renae Holland and Rita Holland for helping with the editing of the book. We would like to thank Jacob Breeden of Process Art House for the Cover Design.

Special thanks to Robert McClory Photography for the back cover image, shot at the US Open / ISKA World Martial Arts Championships in Orlando, FL, and Doug Hodel Photography for the inspiration photo for the cover.

Thank you to Mr. Mike Sawyer, Mr. Mike McCoy, Mr. Cory Shafer, and Mr. Chris Lee for their vision and dedication to the martial arts. For providing opportunities via ESPN2 to showcase the martial artists of the world. You four gentlemen opened the initial doors that have led to many opportunities. Thank you!

CHAPTER 1
THE STORIES THAT SHAPE US

"You are not worthy!" Those words spoken to me almost four decades ago still ring in my ears. They were the culmination of many events in my life that not only shaped my future, but the leadership role I would pursue, and the leader I would become."

--Chip Townsend

Each of us goes through a set of experiences in our lives in order to become the people that we are now. We sometimes look at people who have accomplished great things in their life and think, "They are so lucky." We look at the circumstances that surround them and wonder why our lives can't be more like their lives.

The thing that we often miss, though, is that everyone

has a story about how they became themselves. Everyone has those significant events in their life that help to shape them. The truth of the matter, as we see it, is that it really isn't even those events and experiences that shape us. It is what we do with the experiences that we face and the stories we tell ourselves that define us. I want to start this book by telling you a little bit about who I am. And, I want to preface that by saying that both Jody and I will be telling our stories in helping you to identify your story for yourself. How you define the things that happen in your life is how you create the persona that you become.

Chip's Story

A Trip to the Grocery Store Changes Everything

I was an average kid in an average family. My dad was a welder and he was very good at what he did. My mom was a loving but fiery person. She had four older brothers and one older sister that were more than a little outspoken and always willing to stand up for what they thought. My mom's brothers were put into boxing gloves and allowed to "box out" their issues at times and taught the sport by my grandfather. Because of how direct they were and how aggressive they could be at times, my mom became a very strong person. The strength that she developed in her formative years ended up being a big part of the catalyst for me becoming who I am today.

The first several years of my life, I was a daddy's boy. I loved going anywhere that my father went. If he would let me go to the grocery store, I would go. If he would let me go to a job site, I would go. Dad worked very hard to provide a good home and a good life for us. His work ethic and absolute belief that he can figure anything out if he puts his mind to it still inspire me today. It is amazing to me how much of life I can remember all the way back to the age of 3.

When I was three years old, my dad had purchased a new welding truck. He spent a lot of time getting it set up just the way that he wanted it. He was equipping it with the right tanks, the right toolboxes, and even wiring in his own wench. He had carefully cut a hole in the floorboard of the truck in order to set the wench the way it would be the most functional.

He worked all day on the truck and made tremendous progress. As a welder, my dad used 18 inch welding rods, which are brazing heated by a torch, not electrode style rods. I remember playing around in the truck while he was working on it. I was always pretty good at keeping myself entertained. There was a bundle of those 18 inch rods sitting in the passenger side floorboard of the truck. As I unbundled them and began playing with them, I remember them being fun because they were sort of flimsy. I could pick one of them up and shake it back and forth and it looked pretty cool. Because I had taken the bundling off, there were a whole bunch of these rods just loose in the floorboard of the truck.

The first significant event in my life that I really remember was that day of playing with those welding rods in my dad's truck. My mom needed something from the grocery store and my dad was going to run get it. My sister, who was five years older than me, was going to go with dad to the grocery store and I wanted to tag along. Dad was always willing for me to go with him and so he let me jump in the truck as well.

This was a time before the seatbelt laws and I normally stood in the truck with my arm around my dad's neck. That was where I felt safe. And, let's face it, a boy standing on a seat next to his dad is just pretty cool. I remember looking down at the floorboard where the hole in the floor was. I thought it looked neat because I could see the road flashing by beneath the truck.

Dad's truck was built for work, not for comfort. So, things bounced around a bit. One of the welding rods, that I had unbundled, somehow or another bounced through the floorboard and went down to the highway. When it hit the pavement, it was like it had hit a trampoline. If you remember, those welding rods were pretty flimsy and would vibrate quite a bit when hit. The rod was too long to go all the way out of the truck before it hit the pavement, so one end had remained inside of the truck, and inside of the hole in the floorboard. When the welding rod came back up through the floor board of the pickup, it came up like a bullet out of a gun. It shot straight up and right next to my father. The problem there was that I was right next to my father.

That welding rod went into my right eye and the vibration of the 18 inch rod made the end of it work back and forth after it hit. In a split second, it shredded my right eye. Looking back at that event, my mom tells me that she knew that God had a great purpose for me. Some people look at an event like that and wonder how any mom could see good in losing an eye. What she saw was the fact that the welding rod did not kill me. Had it gone just a little further in, it would have pierced my brain. If that it happened, it's very likely that my story could have ended at three years old. My mom had the ability to be thankful for what she did have and not just angry for what she didn't have.

What followed that event was a series of surgeries. The doctors first tried to repair my eye and they did their very best. After two surgeries attempting to make things better, they realized that my eye was not going to be any good to me anymore. The next surgery was to remove the eye and prepare the eye socket making it possible for me to get a prosthetic eye. As a 3 year old, none of this was on my to-do list for entertaining myself. Prepping an eye socket for a prosthetic eye meant that there were hundreds of stitches inside of my eye socket. It was extremely irritating, itchy, painful, and basically the opposite of what the average three-year-old wakes up and looks forward to in the morning. These stitches and discomfort led to me spending many hours in my mom's lap where she spoke three very distinct messages into my life. She told me these things over and over again.

1. "You are a gift from God." My mother never once made me feel like a burden as I went through this. She held me every day and showed me that the love of God was meant to be given to me through her. She made me feel like I belonged on this earth. No matter how bad the pain was, she helped me realize that God had put me here for a reason. To this day, I remember to wake up and be thankful for the opportunities that are placed before me.

2. "You're going to grow up to be a different kind of man." My mother was no stranger to seeing her brothers brawl and cause problems at times. She was even used to seeing a lot of other people in this world who chose not to live the way that they should. Telling me every day that I was going to be a different kind of man raised my standards. My dad was extremely good at backing up those positive

messages that my mother was giving me. She told me over and over again that I would be the kind of man that other people would want to be.

I have always known that she was watching and expecting me to set an example for others. I still strive every day to be the different kind of man that she spoke of. She imprinted these two p's on my young mind: P-provider and P- protector and she laid a foundation for these "P's" to flourish.

3. "You are going to change this world." I believe with all of my heart that each of us is put on this earth to fulfill a purpose. It may not always be the purpose that is popular or the one that is easy, but it is a purpose. With everything that I have done, from the age of three on, my mom has pushed me to be a leader. I believe that I began thinking at the age of three that leaders can and should change things. I also believed that leaders change things for the good of all and not just for themselves.

Those lessons helped me tremendously to stay focused on what mattered. During my early years of development, it was learning to deal with bullies and learning to function with this "different advantage" that I had over other two eyed folks!

Sneezes and Second Grade

My eye was originally built to last, so it was bigger

than it needed to be when I was young. This meant that things like sneezing affected me significantly different than it did other people. There was a very high likelihood that my eye would fall out when I sneezed. When it did, other kids would laugh and make fun of me. Looking back, I doubt that they were thinking about how their laughs would affect me. I know that I was sure thinking about it at the time, though.

During the first two years of school, I did great. I made all good grades in academics and in kindergarten and first grade. I think most people made awesome grades in nap time, but I really did do well in school and even enjoyed the learning. Second grade was different though. This was my next lesson in leadership.

My second grade teacher looked at my lack of full vision as such a hindrance that she couldn't see me ever making it out of school or amounting to anything. Helen Keller said, "The only thing worse than being blind is having sight but no vision." This teacher had no vision for who I could become and no faith in my will to overcome. She told my mom in a phone conversation that I was going to be a high school dropout and amount to nothing in the future. I remember thinking at 7 years old how awful it was to speak despair into someone's life. It pains me today to think about other kids that she might have told that they were going to fail. How many of those kids believed her?

I am thankful again for the fiery spirit that my mom had then and still has today. She refused to accept the negativity from the teacher and continued to encourage me. That was a rough year and really helped to shape my philosophy of encouragement. When I hit third grade, I had a positive teacher again and everything began clicking like it was supposed to. I worked hard and really did well for the rest of my education through high school.

Thanks to the Bully

In 7th grade, I remember being in the health check line to see the nurse. Do they still do those? Anyway, the kid in front of me was the kid that had been so good at earlier grades that he had been given the opportunity to repeat them a few times. He was a lot bigger than most and operated out of brawn, not brain. Being a couple of years older than I was in 7th grade, he made his mark in the school by bullying kids. If a kid had a weakness, he would find it and exploit it.

With a name like "Chip" in West Texas, the home of "cow chips", and having a prosthetic eye, he had no problem finding a "weakness" to exploit. Without any provocation, while standing in the health check line, he turned to me and told me that he was going to knock my other eye out. That scared me, but not so much from the angle of being afraid of him. It scared me to realize that I really wasn't sure how to defend myself.

That was the year that I started studying martial arts. I had been groomed to fight with tough uncles and a strong father, but I didn't really know how I would defend myself against this guy. One of my uncles was even a professional boxer, so the genetics were in place. My mom wanted me to be a pro boxer, but the boxing coaches wouldn't let me participate because of my prosthetic eye. I wasn't even allowed to try out for tee-ball because of the fear that adults had of me getting injured further. I had been interested in the pictures in the karate books from the book-mobile. I hadn't really seen any Bruce Lee or Chuck Norris movies though. We didn't watch a lot of TV out in the country, where I grew up. (That was in the days when kids didn't use a remote control, they WERE the remote.)

I just had this natural inclination to think that martial arts was cool. That event, even though it could be seen as negative, was the push that got me to join martial arts. So, really, I am thankful for that bully. His words started something that truly changed me forever.

Becoming a Protector

When I visited the gym, I wasn't told that I couldn't participate because of my prosthetic eye. I was encouraged to participate. This showed me in 7th grade that martial arts was designed to help people, even me, to break through barriers.

In high school, I found myself standing up for other kids who were getting pushed around or being bullied. I wasn't really social. I preferred to stay to myself, likely because of the self-conscious feeling of not fitting in due to the amount of bullying that I had been subjected to growing up. I wasn't a football, basketball, or track star, which were the three things in rural Texas that mattered. I, therefore, didn't fit in with the popular kids. Having been subjected to ridicule by others, I knew that bullying was wrong and I knew that I should and could stand up for those who were being picked on. Martial arts helped me to develop the confidence that I needed to stand up for others and to do the right thing when it really mattered.

That desire to defend and to be the best just intensified as I went through high school. I had thought that being in the military would be one of the best ways that I could push myself. The advice that well-intentioned adults had given me repeatedly was that it would be best to join the Air Force or the Army, and maybe the Navy, but not the Marines. The marines pushed harder and they were always the first ones in and the last ones out. For me, that wasn't a deterrent, that was EXACTLY what I wanted to be.

Because I had developed myself into a fighter and because I always wanted to see how far I could push myself, the Marines are what made the most sense in my mind. I had spoken to a couple of recruiters on the phone about what being a Marine would be like, but I had not spoken to any of them in person. I was pretty sure that I either wanted to be Marine recon or a Navy Seal, the best of the best. I knew that I could push myself hard enough to achieve that.

When I was 17 years old, I was walking through the Mall of Abilene and I met a Marine recruiter. I remember that his last name was Ulysses. It seemed like a very different and very military name to me. Working for my dad, I had been driving fork lifts, trucks, and heavy equipment since I was 9 years old. I had earned my black belt and I was more confident than I had ever been in my life. I knew that I could be a Marine. I walked up to him and the conversation went like this.

"Hello sir. My name is Chip Townsend and I'm interested in being a Marine."

He became very excited about a willing recruit and launched into his pitch. "Being a Marine is one of the most honorable things that you could achieve in your life. We are the toughest of the military branches. You will have the opportunity to serve your country and position yourself for success in life. You will be able to be anything that you want to be because of the Marines." He went on for a while about the benefits of being a Marine. I had been told by several civilians that it could be a problem to get into the military because of my prosthetic eye. So, I let him know about it to see if it was still my opportunity to be anything and anybody that I wanted to be.

"I don't know if this is an issue for the Marines. I know that I have done great in my life so far, but I wanted to let you know that I do have a prosthetic eye from an injury when I was younger."

He looked right at me and said, "You are not worthy to be a Marine." He said this without skipping a beat or batting an eye. That was a crushing blow to me. He literally said the words, "YOU ARE NOT WORTHY." Man did that hurt!

To this brash statement, my seventeen year old shocked and likely cocky response was, "You know, I grew up in the country and I have operated every piece of machinery that you can think of. I have hunted all of my life. There isn't a Marine out there that I couldn't match. It may take me a while and I may have to work harder, but I can match them." With that, I turned and walked away from him.

He stuttered out the words as I walked off, "Hey, hey, hey. You know what. You would make a great Marine." His attempt to recover from what he had said wasn't enough to make me forget that statement. It was permanently etched into my psyche. I've never forgotten it. I never will.

Better Not Bitter

One of the lessons that I learned in high school is that in every interaction that we have with other people, we have the potential to personally leave them better or worse, depending on our choices about how we will interact with them. We don't, however, leave them exactly the same way we found them. There are too many people who have leadership titles and speak negativity and failure into people's lives. I think about what I am telling people and how I am encouraging them.

Breakthrough leadership happens every day and in every interaction. It's like ministry, I'm not just reflecting on God in church, but in every interaction in life, everywhere. You are a leader 24/7 or you are not a leader. It has to be a part of who you are at your core.

I had gone through enough in my life to realize that I was a fighter. I fought my way back at three years old from losing an eye. I fought my way back in 7th grade when I realized that I needed to be able to physically defend myself. I fought my way back when I was told that I wasn't worthy to be a Marine. These circumstances in my life and these significant events pushed me to be more. I knew that I had a choice about how I handled what others did and said to me. My choices did then, and will continue today to guide me to break through the negativities of life. And, my choices always have been and always will be responsible for my successes.

Jody's Story

This book is and should be about the TEAM CHIP leadership philosophy. I just want to add a little perspective from my experiences. I believe that each of us will have between 2 and 5 critical experiences before we turn 18 that will shape us. For me, those events happened at 7 years old, 9 years old, and 16 years old.

I Want To Work For Me

When I was 7, my father allowed me to begin working. He had started working for his dad when he was 5. I was jealous. I loved the idea of working and I still love to work today. My first job lasted only one day. My grandfather, on my mom's side, was a farmer, rancher, and executive. He worked from before the sun was up to after it was down six days a week. I had learned to drive at 5 years old, which was fairly common if you spent much time on a Texas farm.

At the age of 7, my grandfather showed me how to drive a tractor and operate a plow. He put me down in a field and showed me how to make the rounds, then turned me loose. I plowed for 12 hours. It was hot and for the most part, kinda boring. But, I was on that tractor for the 12 hours. The wage that my grandfather paid us for our work was $2 per hour. At the end of the day, he paid me $24, as we had agreed upon. The week before that, I had helped my brother mow a lawn. He is 3 years older than me, so he had been allowed to work for a while. He and I split the money for the 90 minutes of work that we did. We were paid $25 for mowing and edging the lawn, which was mathematically a much better deal for me.

I wasn't upset with my grandfather for the deal that we had made, but I realized that it was a much better deal to be in charge than to be the hired hand. I think it is interesting that I learned my lesson about wanting to be an entrepreneur at the age of 7, and in the first week of working. I also think it is interesting that the other lesson that I learned as a 7 year old was from my 2nd grade math teacher.

2nd Grade Can Be Tough

I learned the power of words as they are spoken into other people's lives. Not long after learning that I prefer to be paid for my results instead of for my time, I started 2nd grade. My math teacher was one of those people that woke up every morning upset that life was continuing. She was grumpy and seemed to get worse as every day progressed. I don't know if there was something wrong in her world, but I do know that she created chaos in other people's lives.

One day in class, I didn't understand what she was asking me to do and I therefore didn't know the answer that she was looking for. When I couldn't answer her, she told me to come to the front of the class. After I got up there, she proceeded to tell the class that I was stupid. She pointed out that I was what stupid looked like. She went on about me being stupid for a minute or so and then sent me back to my seat. I wasn't the only one that she attempted to scar emotionally, but I was one of them. She suggested to my parents and to the school that I was probably "retarded." I still hate that word to this day. I was moved out of her class and put in remedial math where a great teacher told me that there was no real reason for me to be there.

I knew math and I was very good at it. The difference between those two teachers demonstrated the power of communication to me. I resented that mean teacher and struggled any time a person used the word "stupid" or the word "retarded" in reference to me. It was not until I was 35 years old that I learned to re-interpret the event. I reshaped that event to realize that I pushed my self much harder in academics because I was proving to myself over and over that I was really smart.

The Martial Art of Change

The next event that shaped me was in 3rd grade, at the age of 9. I was the smallest kid in class. I don't mean just out of the boys. I mean the smallest kid. I didn't really start growing much until high school. I got picked on, made fun of, and teased because of my size. Teachers had trouble believing that I was in the right grade because I didn't appear to be the same age as the other kids.

In 3rd grade, I mowed the library lawn during the summer. Libby Barker was the librarian and she was an awesome lady. When my buddy and I would finish mowing, she would invite us in and teach us about the stars, or history, or anything that we were interested in. In the basement of the library, Richard Knox taught Tae Kwon Do. The basement windows were just above the ground and the happenings inside were visible to me as I mowed. I loved seeing people kicking and punching. I imagined that if I knew martial arts, people would respect me, even if I was small. I had asked Ms. Barker about the classes because I thought she knew everything. She told me that they charged $25 per month. That was 2 ½ weeks of mowing the library to me.

I begged my parents until they finally gave in and allowed me to join. My dad was and still is a preacher and is against fighting, so this was a big step for him to allow me to participate. He was also a little nervous that I would change religions to an Eastern religion. He was safe in that Richard was Assembly of God and their church was on the South side of town, not in the East. I took the classes very seriously and practiced every day at home. I loved martial arts from the first class that I took. I was naturally flexible and had already developed self discipline, so I fit in well in the school.

What I learned, more than fighting, in that class was to carry myself with confidence. To this day, I believe that martial arts was more valuable to my success than college. I learned to stand up for myself, to respect authority, and to be willing to fight if necessary.

I worked hard at martial arts until I broke my leg in my 1-day football career in 8th grade. Being 72 pounds and getting hit by someone who is 165 pounds lends itself to the category of "things that shouldn't be done." I was in traction in the hospital for 23 days, beginning on the 2nd day of 8th grade and then in a cast for all but 2 weeks of the rest of my 8th grade year. That slowed my progress in martial arts significantly.

It was at the age of 16, though, that the lessons about being honorable really started to come out of me. I had gotten into weight lifting and I had grown a foot by the time I was 15. I did martial arts still and I wasn't afraid to stand up for myself. I had also gotten pretty strong. I was at a football game at Wylie High School in Abilene, TX when I witnessed a friend of mine being bullied by some younger, but much bigger guys. It was two guys pushing around one guy and trying to make him feel bad about himself. I remember walking over, crossing my arms to try to make the muscles show a bit, and then telling them that they would have to face me if they ever messed with my friend again. I didn't know if I could take them both, but I knew that I was willing to get hit. It turns out that they weren't as willing to get hit as I was.

I really didn't think about how the guy I defended would feel. I just knew that it wasn't right to do what they were doing and I was there to do something about it. That act of standing up for my friend started to really shape the way that I saw other people. Most of us need somebody to take a stand for us, or to give us a hand up from time to time. I began really wanting to help other people get ahead in life and to believe in themselves. These themes have remained true for me throughout my life. They have shaped my thoughts on leadership and helped me to realize that breakthrough leadership is about how we carry ourselves every day, not just how we perform in front of a group.

Lessons From The Masters

Each of us has a story to tell. Each of us has significant events that helped to shape our thoughts and beliefs in life. We would challenge you to write down at least three events in your life, before the age of 18, that had an impact on you. We would then challenge you to tell your story to someone that you trust.

When you really want to gain someone's trust, to be able to truly encourage and influence (influence = leadership) them, you need to be vulnerable with them. Share your failures and/or your hard times along with your successes. Being genuine and complete will help you to truly impact people. Give people an example of finding the "positive" outcomes from the negative experiences!

Take a few minutes and write down the three events that helped to shape your current belief systems into what they are now.

1. _____

_____

_____

_____

2. _____

_____

_____

_____

3. _____

_____

_____

_____

It is the story that you tell yourself about these events that shapes your beliefs.

YOUR BREAKTHROUGH!

Now, if you don't like the story, "rewrite" it. If the events in your life left you weaker instead of stronger, how could you relook at the story to be one that built you up instead of being one that tore you down? Can you find some golden nuggets of positive in the story that you can share, not to embellish the story, but to make it shine in a positive light?

Take the next page and make some notes on how you grew or became stronger because of these events.

_____

_____

_____

_____

_____

_____

_____

_____

_____

_____

_____

_____

_____

_____

_____

CHAPTER 2
THE PHILOSOPHY

It isn't having a black belt that matters. It is **being** a black belt that matters. Just having a black belt insinuates having a title or position, and depending on it to make you something.

Remember that a black belt is a white belt that never quit!

Check out the Team Chip blog on being a BL.A.C.K. B.E.L.T. :
http://teamchiptkd.wordpress.com/2011/08/19/what-is-a-black-belt/

Perspective from Chip Townsend: Martial arts is more than kicking and punching. It is more than the physical exertion that we submit ourselves to. It is the way in which we carry ourselves. It is who we are at our core in every situation. Martial arts is a way of living.

When I was young and began studying martial arts, it was an outlet that matched my intensity. It was just the right breakthrough for me as a young boy who was already accustomed to fighting for my survival amongst my peer group. It was my motivator to be a success and to be a part of something incredible. I believe that Martial Arts would be the reason for my success, even if I wasn't a professional Martial Artist. I believe this because I learned three keys to success as I began studying Martial Arts in Abilene, TX.

3 Keys to Success

1. Conceive it. Believe it. Achieve it! - The fight is in your mind and in your heart first. As martial artists, we need to know that we can push our bodies further than normal people can. I think that is the reason that I was so attracted to the Marines, and particularly the Seals. They pushed themselves further and harder than anyone else. They understood that if they believed they could keep going in their minds, then they did. Martial Arts is the same way. We work hard every day to be better than we were yesterday.

I push myself to break records for the simple fact that I have to know whether or not it can be done. At one point in history, it was deemed physically impossible to run a 4-minute mile. The day after it was announced that it could not ever be done, it was done by Roger Bannister, at the age of 25. There is a laundry list of people who ventured past the possible into the impossible to see how far we can really go as humans. I believe the first key I learned in Martial Arts is that <u>we have to be able to believe in the impossible before it can be made possible.</u> We have to see it in our mind's eye and then create belief in it. In the words of Audrey Hepburn, "Nothing is impossible; the word itself says I'm possible!"

2. Maintain Upmost Respect - How you do anything is how you do everything. I learned very early on that being respectful is something that is required at all times, not just when I was on the mat. I am thankful that my parents had already taught me this by the time I started martial arts. I am also thankful that my dad and mom both pushed me to perform at my very best in everything that I did. I remember my dad telling me that I needed to work hard now so that I would know how to work hard later, but I would likely not have to work harder later also. They used their own wording, but they got the message across that how I did school would be how I did life. How I did Martial Arts would be how I did life.

The thing that I have noticed over the years is a shift in that mentality in young people. I'm not fully sure if it is because parents are busier now than before and, therefore, don't hold their kids as accountable, or if it is something else. But, I do know that after years of teaching, I get to regularly observe parents. I believe that in an effort to make their kids lives great, they often make excuse after excuse for their children. They put them on pills, buy the electronic babysitters, and jump in to save them from difficulty entirely too soon. Many of them allow their kids to quit any activity at the first sign of difficulty or if it is not "fun" today.

What I do know is that when I get a young man or a young woman in my school (and all ages of adults), they learn to choose success at the highest level. They learn to raise their standards. And, their parents notice. Little Johnny begins to say "yes sir" and "yes ma'am" when he interacts with his parents and teachers.

The key here is that they respect authority because they have learned to really respect themselves. I drill into them that it is their choice to live life at the highest level or their choice not to do so. I also let them know what my standards are and what the standards of my school are. If any student, regardless of age, continuously chooses to live a so-so life in the gym, I know they are living that same so-so life outside of the gym. <u>How we do anything is how we do everything</u>!

3. Don't Stop Learning - You are never done. There is no stopping point in Martial Arts. There isn't a level where you know everything and can do everything. Martial Arts philosophy/structure is not about the destination. It is about continuous improvement. It is about journeying into the impossible to make it possible, then working hard and going to a new impossible place.

    It is a lifestyle that you choose to live into. It is who you are in every moment of every day. In order to be better today, you have to be better than who you were yesterday. That isn't easy for a lot of people. Society seems to be telling people that good enough really is good enough. You shouldn't have to work harder. I disagree! I have faced challenge after challenge in my life and I believe that it is the challenge that has pushed me to work harder and harder.

    I believe that each of us has more to offer the world if we believe that we can improve a little today over where we were yesterday. By believing that I could improve and believing that I could take control of my life, I am not the boy who lost his eye. I am the man who makes great efforts to set an example for others to follow. I am the man who holds

more than a dozen world records and titles. I
am the man that my mother saw as she held
me at the age of 3. I am that man, but I'm
not done yet. <u>We are never done!</u>

--Chip Townsend

Perspective from Jody Holland: I work with
organizations of all sizes to help them create cultures
of success. One of the most frustrating things that
companies seem to be facing, and this has been a
constant for more than a decade, is that of a value
shift in younger workers.

Our society has created an "everyone wins" model,
which in theory sounds pretty good. The challenge is
that young people are not being told when they are
actually doing things wrong. Instead, they are being
told that everything that they do is great and that they
can't be wrong. The real downside of this is that
these people will eventually go to work. They will
find themselves frustrated with the new reality that
their boss doesn't see them as special as their parents
did. They will be expected to work hard, perform,
and get results. They will not be able to simply show
up, get their ribbon, and go home.

I have watched the young people that grow up with a
martial arts instructor that pushes them. The
difference in their level of respect, their work ethic,
and their ability to succeed in life is mind-boggling.

Young people who learn work ethic, integrity,
teamwork, reliability, and other key values will learn

most of them before the age of 14, or their freshman year in high school. They will learn these values based on what they are exposed to and what is expected of them.

Martial Arts, particularly Team Chip TKD, has been incredible at pushing, motivating, and inspiring young people to choose the right path in life. Young people who are in a great martial arts school are expected to be respectful to their teachers and parents. They are expected to make good grades and always do their best. These solid expectations condition young people to believe that they should behave in that way. It is their belief that leads to their thoughts. It is their thoughts that lead to their attitudes. It is their attitudes that determine their behaviors. And, it is their behaviors that lead to their outcomes.

Young people will naturally test the limits of what they can get away with. That is a part of psychological development. It is not the fact that they test adults that is bad. It is the fact that adults often lower the standards of the "test" instead of raising them for young people. A great Martial Arts program will raise a young person's standards and propel them into a better life. A sword cannot be sharpened without the abrasion of a stone. Gold cannot be purified without fire. And young people cannot become the best version of themselves without being pushed. The same is true for adults.

If we intend to be more, do more, and have more, then we have to be willing to be pushed. The reason that I have been so excited about this book for the last two years is that I have seen the TEAM CHIP model of success reshape people's lives. The side benefit was that they became incredible martial artists in the process.

When I was 9 years old, Sang Ju Cho, my senior instructor, told us that it was the learning of martial arts philosophy, more than the physical mastery of a skill, that would shape our lives. He was right. Master Chip has simply been able to distill that information into an incredible acronym.

--Jody Holland

We have been talking about putting this book together for almost two years now. We both believe that the world is looking for, even craving, a way to live their lives with more honor. Martial arts has been an integral part of both of our lives and has helped to shape the philosophies that we live by. Neither of us were Texas football stars. For one reason or another, we both ended up feeling a little "outside" of the norm for our schools. Martial arts accepted us, pushed us, and challenged us to be more, to do more, and ultimately to have more in life. The philosophy of achievement began with a philosophy of belief. We would like to share some perspectives that we believe will help make the TEAM CHIP model make the most sense.

Lessons From the Masters

It is who you become that determines what you do. We have seen that the philosophy of a master must be demonstrated in every act and in every moment. Leadership is not about a big event or some incredible change that is created. Leadership is about the way in which we live…daily.

Martial Arts is one of the best platforms for developing good values in young people and reshaping misguided values in adults. There is nothing like sharing your martial arts gift via a strong, crisp demonstration of technique that inspires some awe, and gets the undivided attention of a group of people. By being the best version of yourself as a martial artist and a leader, you are taking a step in the direction of gaining the students' true respect, which leads to gaining their trust to follow you to a great destination. When they are inspired to follow a great example, then their journey of constant improvement has truly begun! The philosophy of a Martial Artist is the precursor to the way in which they will behave on and off the mat. By becoming the right person, the skills of the artist are honed.

Each and every day, in every workout, in every fight, we make a choice. We choose who we are, what we will be, and how far we can and will push ourselves. We win in the ring when we have first won in our own minds. We break through barriers when we begin to believe that there is no such thing as "impossible."

YOUR BREAKTHROUGH!

In order to be the person that you were always intended to be, you will have to define yourself. Too many people in this world wander through life trying to find themselves. It is your time to define who you will be for the rest of your life. Take the next page and write out what your top 3 guiding values are and how you will use those values to live your life as a breakthrough leader. We also encourage you to take a moment and let other people know that you are on this journey. By letting others know that you are striving to live a breakthrough leadership life, you create personal accountability for your growth. Post something on Facebook with the hashtag: #breakthroughleadership .

_____

_____

_____

_____

_____

_____

_____

_____

_____

_____

_____

_____

_____

_____

_____

_____

_____

_____

_____

_____

_____

NOW LET'S BEGIN A T.E.A.M. C.H.I.P.
BREAKTHROUGH LEADERSHIP JOURNEY
TOGETHER!

CHAPTER 3
T IS FOR TEACHABLE

Teachable *He taught me and said to me, "Let your heart hold fast my words; keep my commandments, and live. Get wisdom; get insight; do not forget, and do not turn away from the words of my mouth. (Proverbs 4:4, 5 ESV)*

"Be willing to be a beginner every single morning."
Meister Eckhart

Just when you think you know all the answers, someone will change the questions. This truth, I am sure, has been spoken and/or revealed in multiple settings for each of us. In school, we strive to know the answers. We believe that there is always a right answer. We do our lessons and study for the test. In school, we are given the information to master and then, only after we have been given the information, we take the test. Life isn't quite like that. In life, many times we are given the test, and then we are given the information/lesson. We fail the test and either give up (end of the journey) or we work harder and take a new test again and again, until the day that we realize that we are focusing on the wrong teacher. We are trying to learn only from the teacher in charge.

Life tests us all differently. We are tested from information that we gather from children, from nature, and from every aspect of life. To be teachable, we have to be looking for the answers everywhere we turn, maybe not just from the person who presents themselves as the teacher. We have to be humble and open to learning from anywhere above us, below us, in front of us, and even behind us.

There have been times for each of us where a child does something that we have never seen before. It's a cool move or a unique kind of attack, or a counter. Wherever they saw it or learned it, the fact remains, it's cool and we haven't seen it before. If we are arrogant, we will tell the kid to do it the way they were taught and to stop thinking on their own. If we are great leaders, though, we ask them to repeat it and we attempt to learn from them. Being teachable is about being open to learn something new in every situation and in every setting. It isn't the stripes on a belt that teach us. It is the person that teaches us. Regardless of whether you are a 6th Degree Black Belt or a Yellow Belt, you have something to offer. Regardless of whether you are a 6th Degree Black Belt or a Yellow Belt, you have something to be taught.

From Chip

Your position in your life or organization is nothing until you get inside that position and make it something. If you are a yellow belt, but you are the best yellow belt in the world, you will make the world a better place. We, at Team Chip, call this act of getting into your position and making the most of it, having a "black belt heart". For instance, from the example above, "I may only be a yellow belt, but I'm going to be the best yellow belt ever".

One afternoon, when I was teaching a group of students, I needed them to get the point that they had something to offer and something to learn, so I took my black belt off. I asked them, "How much is this belt worth?" Students will say things like "a million dollars" and other large amounts of money. I then tell them, "No, right now the belt isn't even holding my pants up. It isn't worth much at all if it is not serving the purpose that it was intended to serve." Then, I put the belt back on and asked them, "Now, what is the belt worth?" They are often confused when I ask them because of what I told them right before that. I then continue, "The belt is worth me at this moment. The belt is worth what I put in it, literally and figuratively. The belt is worth everything if it is a true reflection of my heart. If I am living my life as a teachable student and always seeking to learn, then my <u>belt</u> will be priceless."

Being teachable means remaining open. It means not having to be the one that was always right. In fact, I have found that I am often faced with the choice between being "right" and being "successful." Living a successful life is all about not restricting my lid of learning, not capping myself with the limited mindset of "I'm done, I'm good enough, or I'm finished".

It is about seeking ways to learn in every circumstance. It is operating with a "beginner's mindset." Every day, I think of myself as a beginner who needs to work as diligently as possible to become a master. By not assuming that I have mastered a thing, I am not assuming that I will be great at that thing automatically. I plan to work. I plan to fail. I plan to get back up and work harder than the last time.

When I severed my Achilles tendon in January 2006, I was told that my Martial Arts career was very likely over. I tend to have a stubborn, hard-headed streak that says, "No, I'm not done yet, and I need to find the positive in this perceived negative of being injured." I asked myself several times, "What is the golden nugget that God is showing me here? What can I do to maximize my physical down time during the recovery of this injury?" I believe that there were two key areas where I became teachable from this opportunity. Those two areas were in the development of both <u>wisdom</u> and <u>intelligence</u>.

Wisdom and intelligence are two different types of learning. Wisdom, in my mind, is seeing someone trip over something and thinking, "I'm not going over there and doing the same thing as them." Wisdom is learning from the mistakes of others. Intelligence is being the one that tripped and then realizing that I need a new path. I want to be both wise and intelligent. I want to learn from the mistakes that other people make as well as from the mistakes that I make. If I don't have to make all of the mistakes myself and I can learn from the struggles that others have faced, I become wise. This mindset makes me teachable.

Severing my Achille's tendon, mid-performance on a stack of bricks in Atlantic City, NJ, was definitely a "trip." But that experience taught me that when one area suffers, another can flourish. Being wheeled around Ground Zero in a wheelchair, changed my "what am I going to do?" to "what can I do?"

In that period that I was not able to train physically, I knew that I had little eyes on me. I knew that I could make this a teachable moment for my students. So, I went back to college, and earned my Bachelor of Business Administration Degree.

Find the Golden Nugget

One of the problems that we have in our current

society is that of falsely puffing up the self-esteem of young people in a way that is not genuine. We are giving participation ribbons and last place trophies. We are conditioning our kids that they have not failed and they cannot fail. This gives them a false sense of security and sets them up for real failure when they face problems later in life. Napoleon Hill, in his book <u>Think and Grow Rich</u> said, "In every problem lies the seed of an equivalent benefit." Hill went on to explain that we had to be open to learn the lessons that were there before that "seed of an equivalent benefit" would show itself to us.

I want to find the seeds of success in every challenge. I do have to actually face the challenge, though, in order to receive the benefit. And, like Hill said, the benefit is equivalent. This means that as we face and overcome tougher and tougher challenges, all the while modeling for our children how to work through problems with a teachable mindset, the benefits become greater.

Blog Link For Teachable:
http://teamchiptkd.wordpress.com/2013/01/15/teachable/

From Jody

When I was a sophomore in college, I told my English Literature teacher that I wanted to be an expert in English Lit. She perked up and then asked me, "Are you sure you are willing to learn?" "Of course I am!" I responded with confidence. She said, "Alright, then you will need to read at least 100 books on the subject. Then, you will be ready to be a master and learn from another 100 books."

When I received my 1ˢᵗ Degree Black Belt, I remember telling my instructor how happy I was that I had arrived. He let a smirk come across his face and he said, "I am glad that you are finally at the starting line as well." My heart sank a little as I thought about the fact that the more than a decade of Martial Arts did not mean that I could now beat Bruce Lee (Assuming he came back to life to face me). It meant that I was ready to BE the black belt, and not just to wear the belt.

Over the years, I have focused on developing a "What's Next" mentality. My belief is that there is always something that is next, that is bigger, that is more than I have already demonstrated. This philosophy of "What's Next" has pushed me to exceed my limitations and has forced me to learn something new on a regular basis. It has forced me to remain teachable in life. Joseph Murphy, in his book, The Power of The Subconscious Mind, explains the incredible power that our thought life has on us.

When we think that we always have something new to learn, then we tend to be continuously seeking something new. In every book that I read, in every seminar that I attend, in every moment of my life, I strive to find a golden nugget of wisdom. Like Chip said, we must strive to be both wise and intelligent.

TEACHABLE QUOTE

"A winner knows how much he still has to learn, even when he is considered an expert by others.
A loser wants to be considered an expert by others, before he has learned enough to know how little he knows."

--Sydney J. Harris

Lessons From the Masters

First, Being teachable is fully a choice. ANYONE can choose to open their mind and learn, or close it and limit themselves to "good enough".

Second, many times, being teachable can be a matter of putting your pride behind you, accepting your humanity (imperfection) and seeking input. Being teachable is about learning that learning can and will come from all directions. It will come from the younger, the older, the inexperienced, the experienced, and at times it will come when you least expect it. Learning comes from ALL directions in life.

Third, great lessons will come when you least expect them. You need to be willingly and eagerly searching for more knowledge, more information, more wisdom, and more guidance at all times.

YOUR BREAKTHROUGH!

We would like for you to take a moment, search deep within, and write down three of your personal barriers to choosing to be teachable, as well as what you can do to break through those barriers:

1. _____

_____

_____

_____

2. _____

_____

_____

_____

3. _____

_____

_____

_____

Next, take a moment to think through the idea that you are allowing your pride to block your willingness to learn from anywhere. This part may be very difficult, but total honesty with yourself generally is. When done well, this exercise in thinking through this area, should help open your eyes to new learning opportunities that are presented to you each day.

Now, we've chosen to open our mind to learning from even the most unexpected places. Let's get out there and set the example of willingly, and excitedly looking for opportunities to learn and grow. Take a moment to write out where you will strive to be teachable in the next week. We would encourage you to post what you are going to do. Make sure that you use #breakthroughleadership in your post.

_____

_____

_____

_____

_____

_____

_____

_____

_____

_____

_____

_____

_____

_____

_____

_____

_____

_____

_____

_____

_____

_____

_____

_____

CHAPTER 4
E IS FOR EXCELLENT

 Excellence

Finally, brothers, whatever is true, whatever is honorable, whatever is just, whatever is pure, whatever is lovely, whatever is commendable, if there is any excellence, if there is anything worthy of praise, think about these things. (Philippians 4:8 ESV)

"We are what we repeatedly do. Excellence, then, is not an act, but a habit."
--Aristotle

"The quality of a man's life is in direct proportion to his commitment to excellence, regardless of his chosen field of endeavor."
--Vince Lombardi

Excellence always begins with you being excellent, living it no matter what. Regardless of whether you are executing a sidekick, leading a meeting, or making a sandwich. Living with your utmost excellence truly matters. John Maxwell said in his book, 21 Irrefutable Laws of Leadership, that leadership, at its essence, is influence. "If you believe you are a leader and turn around to see that no one is following, then you are just out taking a walk." In everything that we do, we are demonstrating the core of who we are. This means exactly what Aristotle was referencing. Becoming excellent at anything that we do means that we create a habit of being excellent from the inside out with our daily activities and habits.

When you live life at your very best, you will attract people to you. Think about the leaders in your life that have influenced you the most. They are the ones that live their lives at a higher level. They are the ones that you look up to and reference when you are trying to make important decisions. The best leaders are not focused on being leaders. They are focused on breaking through barriers and unlocking the potential that they have inside of them. By living life as an example, we inspire others to take action in the right direction.

Could You Make a Change in 7 Days?

What if you made the choice to think only positive thoughts and say only positive things for seven consecutive days? What if you decided to be a positive influence within your environment? What difference do you think that would make for the people around you? A big part of living life at your very best is looking for the very best in life. We want to make this challenge to you... For seven straight days, think only positive thoughts and say only positive things. If during that seven days, you mess up and think negatively or say negative things, simply start again at that exact moment. It may take you a full year to have seven consecutive days of thinking excellent thoughts. That's okay! It will very likely be the best year of your life. To be an excellent person, you start with thinking in terms of excellence.

Your thought life will create the rest of your life. It is your inner world that creates your outer world. When it comes to being excellent, you must see yourself as excellent. You must tell yourself that you live with excellence. You must convince yourself that a subconscious level that being excellent is simply a part of who you are. The rest of what we talk about in this book is dependent upon you getting this one component. At the end of every day, I want you to write down three things that you did that were excellent for that day. Let's start with a little practice. In the last 24 hours, what are three things that you did that were great accomplishments? How did you demonstrate your excellence? Take a minute and write those down in the space provided.

Three things that I did in the last 24 hours that demonstrated excellence:

1. _____

2. _____

3. _____

Ensuring that we have three excellent things to say about ourselves at the end of each day is one of the ways that we make sure that we focus on excellence. It's a really good idea that you write out those three things before you go to bed each night. Each person needs to take the time to condition themselves towards excellence, from the inside out.

It isn't just how we demonstrate leadership. It is how we live leadership. Living a life of excellence means that we focus on creating incredible relationships. It means that we truly care about the people that are around us. It means that we demonstrate through our actions who we are.

From Chip

When you think about how you do a sidekick in Tae Kwon Do, you get a mental image of the way that you lift your leg, pivot, rotate your hip, pull your knee back across your chest, explosively extend your leg, and execute the strike. You can see yourself pulling your leg back, rotating your hip, pivoting back, and lowering your leg. You try to combine the perfect mental imagery of the sidekick with the perfect physical execution of the sidekick. You visualize the timing that you use in executing the sidekick as your attacker rushes towards you. You visualize striking at the perfect moment and in the perfect spot in order to stop your attacker. You visualize this kick over and over again. You execute this kick over and over again. You do this so often that performing the kick perfectly simply becomes a natural extension of who you are. You are moving yourself through the stages of learning to the point of excellence. When you have achieved excellence, it becomes simply a knowing. The kick is simply a part of who you are, not just what you do, it is you. This is the physical essence that drives people to live in thought excellence.

From Both of Us

The world has changed its standards and has seemed to lower its expectations for performance. As more and more people type and fewer people write things in longhand, schools have begun to relax on the idea of teaching cursive.

When we were growing up, being able to write with cursive and execute the letters the way that they were supposed to be written helped to teach us a valuable lesson. The lesson really didn't have anything to do with our actual handwriting, though. The lesson had to do with our ability to discipline ourselves to do the right things in the right way. Each week, we were expected to raise our standards and improve our work product. Teachers pushed us hard to perform at our personal best. We believe that martial arts helps to fill a gap that seems to be missing in society today when it comes to detail execution.

Ten THOUSAND Hours

"Our ability to be truly excellent as a teacher is a direct reflection of our ability to disguise repetition as engaging work." --Chip Townsend

For someone to truly master a specific skill set, they need 2500 correct repetitions at a minimum. To be considered a master, they would need 10,000 hours of practice. Malcolm Gladwell, in his book Outliers, tells a story of Bill Gates and the 10,000+ hours that he spent coding before he started Microsoft. In each of the stories that Gladwell relates in that book, the people who became masters spent that amount of time dedicated and focused on building success in one specific area.

We have to be willing to do the same thing. Whether it means executing the perfect roundhouse kick 2500 times in one month or focusing on how we develop our own breakthrough leadership skills for five years, ten years, or more, excellence requires discipline. Our job, as we see it, is to set our personal bar as high as possible so that others will want to follow.

We don't want to be the one that is easily caught in any area of our life. We strive to be so good that others sit around thinking about how they can advance to the same level. This isn't to say that we're arrogant or cocky. The truth is, we want to beat who we were yesterday. And tomorrow, we'll want to beat the person that we were today. Being excellent means living in a cycle of continuous and never-ending improvement, focused on self first and then potentially others.

What Cycle Do You Live In?

Dr. Edwards Deming, who helped rebuild Japan after World War II was an American scholar to introduce the concept of constant and never-ending improvement into business. The interesting thing was, he wasn't that well accepted in the United States. The Japanese people needed someone to help them figure out how to get on their feet after World War II. Their entire country had been decimated. The technology was so bad in Japan during that time, that you could barely send the telegraph.

With the concepts that Deming introduced, the Japanese people developed a philosophy that they refer to is kaizen. That Japanese word simply means continuous improvement. Excellence is the cycle that you live in. It is the improvement that you make today over yesterday and tomorrow over today. It is how we create exponential growth in a martial art school or in a business. When you live life at full volume, people want to come out and hear what you have to say. Being excellent means being 100% of what you're capable of being.

Abraham Maslow said, "If you intentionally become less than you are capable of being, then I warn you, you will be unhappy for the rest of your life." Who in this world would intentionally become less than they are capable of being? We would argue that most people would. How many people have you known that had tremendous talent, all the capabilities in the world, yet they didn't have the drive or discipline to maximize those talents?

When you live life with excellence, you are always driving to deliver. An excellent leader does not hold back. Don't hold anything back in life! Live your life with excellence!

EXCELLENCE QUOTES

"If a man is called to be a street sweeper, he should sweep streets even as a Michelangelo painted, or Beethoven composed music or Shakespeare wrote poetry. He should sweep streets so well that all the hosts of heaven and earth will pause to say, 'Here lived a great street sweeper who did his job well."
                                   --Martin Luther King Jr.

Pepperdine University Sociology Professor John Johnston makes a distinction between EXCELLENCE and mere success:

Success bases its worth on a comparison with others. Excellence gauges our value by measuring us against our own potential.

Success grants rewards to the few but is the dream of the multitudes. Excellence is available to all living beings but is accepted by the few.

Success focuses its attention on the external, becoming the taste-maker for the insatiable appetites of the consumer. Excellence beams a spotlight on the internal spirit, excellence cultivates principles and consistency."

Lessons From the Masters

Excellence is a choice that we make in everything that we do. Choose wisely.

To be personally excellent means giving your best at all times. Excellence has to be the focus even on those menial task that seem to be unimportant. This is even more important as a breakthrough leader. What kind of example do you want your family, children, employees, co-workers, teams, etc. to see?

YOUR BREAKTHROUGH!

The next time you are thinking about training (I'm thinking in terms of working out / martial arts, but this could be applied to any scenario), contemplate this lesson that Chip's mom taught him many years ago when he was a young child:

> Your body is a temple. It's God's temple. Jesus is with you every day in your heart. He makes your body His home. Now, with that in mind, do you want Jesus living in an outhouse or a mansion?

I don't know about you, but that has been a very powerful charge in my life to be my best, at all times. It reminds me continuously to drive for excellence!

Now, no matter what it is you are about to do, go get it and give it your all, Breakthrough Leadership style!! Don't forget to hold yourself accountable for excellence by letting the world know your plan. Make sure to use #breakthroughleadership in your post.

I will be excellent in the following way:

_____

_____

_____

_____

CHAPTER 5
A IS FOR ACCOUNTABLE

Accountability *Iron sharpens iron, and one man sharpens another. (Proverbs 27:17 ESV)*
And no creature is hidden from his sight, but all are naked and exposed to the eyes of him to whom we must give account. (Hebrews 4:13 ESV)

"Let him that would move the world, first move himself." Socrates

Accountability is about consequences, good or bad. Each of us should be held responsible for our actions. Every action yields a consequence. Good actions yield good consequences. Bad actions yield bad consequences. Whether we realize it or not as leaders, people are always looking at us.

From Chip:

"You can do ANYTHING for 8 seconds."

It was 2008. I had returned to the competition stage after that Severed Achilles' tendon. Remember, I was supposed to be "done"; my career was supposed to be "over". I was competing for the ISKA (International Sport Karate Association) World Ultimate Breaker Title. I had won the title in 2004, defended and retained it in 2005, and then taken two years off due to the Achilles' injury.

The competition consists of four separate divisions, with the scoring based on overall placement in the separate divisions. The competition is set in a way that all breaking skills are displayed: speed, power, creativity, and realism.

After a two year "break," I was the underdog again. Other breakers had taken the top seeding, and I was gunning for the top points again.

The challenge with this type of completion lies in not only maintaining a high level of performance, but in staying focused when you hit a speed bump. A strategic error on my part had me in 2nd place after the first two divisions. If I was going to reclaim the title, and show once and for all that I was not "done", I had to win the final two divisions.

Leaders ALWAYS Have an Audience

In our field of "expertise" we always have an audience looking for that example that we talked about in the chapter on excellence. I remember seeing an interview with Charles Barkley on ESPN. The reporter asked him what he thought about being a role model for young people and whether his behaviors were appropriate. Barkley looked at the reporter and responded with something similar to, "I'm not anybody's role model. I don't want to be a role model. I just want to play basketball." The important lesson that Barkley missed is that anyone that is in a leadership position is going to be seen as a role model.

Some role models are good. Others are not so good. All of them, however, are influencers. When we are held responsible for the choices that we make, we tend to think through those choices more carefully. When we believe that we are not responsible for our own actions, then we tend to take actions that are not good for us or for those who look up to us.

When I went into the third division, I knew what I had to do. I knew that I had eyes on me, wondering if I would get up, or shut down. I threw everything hard. So hard, in fact, that about half way through my routine, I had a break that I perform as bricks are falling. Rather than being stationary, the strike has to be faster than the falling bricks. I saw mid-swing that the bricks had rotated in the fall. I hit them anyway.

I knew it hurt. BAD. But, I continued on through the routine, and cleaned every break. I had won the division. But as I was backstage thinking of the next division, and testing the strength of my right arm, I knew (I had felt this feeling before) my arm was broken.

Order

In a martial arts school, there is a specific order to the way the people are expected to line up in classes. The higher belts, with the most experience and skill, line up in the front, and the belts go in order from highest to lowest from front to back. At Team Chip it is not uncommon to move a higher belt to the back of the class when they are not performing with excellence.

This is because accountability isn't just about "testing day" (in martial arts there is a testing day which is a performance opportunity for the students to try to move up in belt rank after they have fulfilled the requirements of their current belt rank). It is about every day, every act, and every interaction. Creating this level of accountability for top performance at all times helps to remind people that they never really arrive, but continue to grow, they are always on the journey. This is true for all of us. Our journey is a daily set of measurements on our life. At Team Chip we work very hard with each promotion the students earn, to raise the level of personal accountability for that student. We work to get them to see their importance as leaders, based on their class placement, even when they don't realize they are leading. Each student is not only responsible for themselves, but for how the world around them sees martial arts based on them.

Gatekeeper

Also, at Team Chip TKD we have a checks and balances system in place before a student can test for promotion from one belt to another. They must have logged a minimum amount of class hours on the mat, and they must have earned stripes for specific requirements at each belt level. Finally, they must ask for permission to test from a certified instructor, getting the instructor to sign off that they agree that the student is prepared to move forward. This is all intended to help teach and encourage personal accountability on the part of the student and instructors. For the student, they have to ask themselves, "Have I taken all necessary steps to be responsible and prepare for this exam?" For the instructor, many times myself, I have to ask myself, "Have I taken all necessary steps to prepare my students for their next big challenge?"

When I explain this to my students, in an effort to get them to take personal responsibility for their results, I explain to them that I'm only a gatekeeper that gives a final yes or no to them as they ask to enter the "gate" of the next level. I explain that it is fully up to them to get their class hours in, get their stripes earned, to get their other physical and mental requirements accomplished, and it is my job to say yes or no based on what they present to me. If they have been teachable and attacked their training with excellence it should be easy to get a yes from me without any difficulty. In essence, it is up to them to get through the gate, I only monitor the gate.

Handing Over the Keys

Part of the accountability involved in the Testing procedure is knowing that, as a student, you hold the keys. When all of the preparation is in place, you not only know the answers to the questions, but you also know the questions themselves. In essence, you as a student, hold the keys to the gate.

In that final division in 2008, I was required to use both arms, and both legs. The rules stated that in the event of an injury, that a competitor could use a single layer of tape as a support.

When I said to my wife, "my arm is broken." "I don't think I can do this", I really expected a pat on the back, and a hug. Instead, she said, "you've trained too hard, for too long. I know you. You can do anything for 8 seconds."

You see, my wife knew that when the pain subsided, that it would have made me crazy to have gotten so close, and given up. She knew that "quit" wasn't and still isn't in my vocabulary. She was my accountability when I needed it.

What could we accomplish if we had people that instead of jumping on the pity parade, said, "You can do anything for 8 seconds"? What if when we fell down, we had people around us that would not only push us, but pull us.

That year, I experienced something I had never experienced before, and haven't again. I stepped out of the circle of boards, not only winning the division, but establishing a new World Record. I dropped to my knees as the room around me grew black. The previous record was 27 boards in 8 seconds. I broke 36.

Do You Seek Accountability?

Now let's think, how different would it be within an organization, if each person who was promoted to the next level of responsibility, actively sought out additional accountability? Do you think that changing the way in which a person sees their role in the organization would change the way in which they hold themselves accountable?

From Jody

What happens in a lot of organizations is that a person will get promoted and then feel like they should not have to work as hard. The truth of the matter is that more responsibility equals more accountability. We become accountable for our results as well as the results of those who report to us. In martial arts, lower belts report to upper belts. In the corporate or business world, employees report to their supervisors. Upper belts continuously earn the respect of lower belts by being accountable for their actions and setting the right example. Supervisors should continuously earn the respect of employees by being accountable for their actions and setting the right example of excellence. Some of the leaders within organizations that have talked to us about how to get their people to perform at higher levels have used this as a key lesson.

Let's say, for example, the supervisor shows up late to work on a regular basis. This supervisor doesn't clock in or out. They're not actually required to be there by 8 AM. The problem is, their employees are required to be there by 8 AM and they work for an hourly wage instead of a salary. When the supervisor chooses not to demonstrate responsibility and accountability in being timely, he/she makes the choice not to do the right thing much easier for the employee. People don't do what we say, they do what we do.

This premise of living an accountable life has been put to the test in Corporate America as well as in each of the Chip's TKD Centers. At each progressive level, a higher standard is expected, and we must communicate clearly this raised expectation.

One example of this was a supervisor for a healthcare facility that was chronically late. She indicated that she was late because that was simply who she was and she couldn't do anything about it. In talking with her, a specific process was followed to initiate accountability in her. In this process, she was asked to explain her morning and every aspect of what she did. With each activity, the amount of time required for the task was asked of her. She responded on each one and as the time was added up, it was uncovered that she was normally 20 minutes late, and that it took an average of 80 minutes to get ready and get to work. It was also uncovered that she got out of bed an average of 60 minutes before she was supposed to be at work. Instead of "telling her" what to do and how to fix her problem, she was asked a question. "What, in that process, could you do differently that would get us the result of you being on time?" She wasn't told to get up earlier. She might have been able to get ready quicker. She decided that the easiest thing would be to get up earlier. She was then asked to explain what she was going to do in order to accomplish this objective of being on time every time.

Components of Accountability

If you followed that sequence, there were three basic components, or questions, that were followed. When these are followed in this way and in this order, they produce personal accountability the vast majority of the time. The three questions were...

> 1. Walk me through the steps of what happened from start to finish.
>
> 2. At what point could you have made a different decision that would have gotten us the result that we needed instead of the result that we got?
>
> 3. What will you put into place for the future to ensure that we get the right result the first time and every time?

Whether it is knowing the tenets of Tae Kwon Do or mastering each of the forms through your belt level, you are responsible for the outcomes that you generate.

Finish the following sentence.

To me, accountability is: _____

_____

The word, accountable, originates from the 14th Century and means, "answerable," literally "liable to be called to account." To be liable to be called to account means that, at any moment, you must be able to demonstrate your preparedness. As a leader, you are cumulatively responsible for your success and the knowledge that you have acquired. You must answer for each and every choice. We take a risk as a leader. You put yourself out there. You make yourself answerable to the people that you lead as well as to the people that you follow. One of the most effective ways to sum this up is in the following statement.

You are exactly who you are and exactly where you are because of the exact choices that you have made. It is not anyone else's fault. You have a choice.

There's Power in the Choice: You

This is a tough pill for lots of people to swallow. We want to blame circumstances. We want to blame the things that happen to us that were not a part of our plan. We want to wallow in self-pity or say that we're too tired, or that we didn't have the right advantage. The truth is, we have a choice in every situation that we face. What we choose in each situation will determine what we get in each next segment of our life. We are accountable for the development of our people. We are accountable for the success of our organizations. We are accountable for the example that we provide for others to follow. We are accountable for each of the results that we get in life.

Give us a Break!

Imagine the level of commitment and accountability that is required when executing a break. If you are going to break a board, a brick, or even a bat, you have to be willing to be "all in." As a breakthrough leader, you put everything that you have into what you are doing in that moment. You live in the now. The past is behind you and the future is yet to be written, but the present moment is what you have and what you are responsible for. Each break that you execute requires you to be fully accountable for your technique, your action, and yourself.

Learning to breakthrough, you become willing to accept even the negative consequences of wrong technique. If you were to try to break a bat with a roundhouse kick and the bat didn't break, you can't blame the bat. You have to accept that you did not do something right. The exact same thing is true as you master leadership. Your job is to break through barriers with your people and inspire them to want to produce more. If you are not getting the results that you desire out of your life, begin by examining what else you need to learn, or what techniques you need to master. When you fully accept responsibility for yourself in each successive moment of life, then... You are accountable.

ACCOUNTABLE QUOTE

"You cannot escape the responsibility of tomorrow by evading it today." Abraham Lincoln

Lessons From the Masters

Choose to be accountable. Don't blame anyone else for your situation in life. You may not like where you are and you may have intended to be somewhere else, but you are here. So, ask yourself the following in any situation that you find yourself in:

In this situation, with the resources that I have, what can I do to make it better?

Being accountable is about being empowered to own your choices. It is so empowering when you grasp that you do have the ability to change the situation, or at least the way you respond to it.

Accountability will always lead to consequences. Some consequences are good and they are sought after. Some consequences are bad and they are to be prevented.

It doesn't matter if it is good or bad. What matters is what standard you hold yourself to now.

Accountability as a martial artist is proven when you execute a technique in breaking, in defending yourself, or in the way in which you lead your class. It is always the result that you get from being fully accountable for your actions.

YOUR BREAKTHROUGH!

Ask yourself the following questions and honestly contemplate your feelings and thoughts here:

Are you making daily choices that make you feel strong? For the next 21 days, break through barriers by starting your day with a positive affirmation. An example would be: "Today is going to rock!" Write out the affirmation that you will commit to for the next 21 days here:

_____

_____

Do you willingly own up to and accept the results of your poor results when you have them? Are you learning and growing from those results? Is there a recent poor result that you have had in life that you did not fully accept responsibility for? Go own up to that responsibility now, and enjoy the empowered feeling of holding yourself accountable.

Are you regularly reviewing your personal standards? Take a few minutes and write out the ideal you. Look at the list and ask yourself what steps you need to take to achieve this ideal you. Start taking the steps now! Find an accountability partner, someone you trust to tell about your mission to be the ideal you. This can be a new beginning to your conscious effort to be the best you possible!

Ready, set, go!! Attack this activity!

The list of attributes that will make me the ideal person and help me to be accountable for succeeding...

_____

_____

_____

_____

_____

_____

_____

_____

_____

CHAPTER 6
M IS FOR MOTIVATED

 Motivation *But Jesus looked*

at them and said, "With man this is impossible, but with God all things are possible." (Matthew 19:26 ESV)

"Ability is what you're capable of doing.
Motivation determines what you do. Attitude
determines how well you do it."
--Lou Holtz

Motivation is one of those tricky subjects that people often misunderstand. Your job as a leader is to create an environment of motivation. The problem is that motivation, at its essence, isn't an external event. Motivation is an internal state that each person must learn to achieve on their own. "People often say that motivation doesn't last. Well, neither does bathing. That's why we recommend it daily." – Zig Ziglar

Motivation is connected to the emotional interpretation of life, at that moment, for that person. This makes it subjective, not objective. In looking at this word, "motive" is "to be brought forward, a reason for action," or the Latin "motus – motion." Motivation is to be in motion with a specific reason backing up that motion.

Abraham Maslow has been considered the father of motivation theory. Maslow defined his "hierarchy of needs" as the reasons, or motives, for people to act in specific ways. He referenced the research observation that there is an order to the motivated action of humans. His theory held that we, as humans, would take action on the most pressing needs in our life in a sequence. We would not focus on higher order needs, until the lower order, more critical needs to the person's survival, were satisfied. This theory indicated that we were virtually incapable of being "self-actualized" if we were fearing for our safety, for example.

As you can see in the pyramid, the base level is our physiological needs, then safety and security, then love and belonging, then self-esteem, then self-actualizing. Maslow indicated that the wider the base (closer to the bottom), the more important the need. This is a very logical theory and has really opened the doors for other researchers and psychologists and leaders to better understand human nature and the nature of motivation. Herzberg developed his "Two-Factor Theory" as a result of Maslow's theory and research. Herzberg realigned what Maslow had said and outlined that there are Hygiene factors and Maintenance factors that can be organized from Maslow's Pyramid. He indicated that there are things that motivate us when they are added and there are other things that demotivate us when they are missing. The internal factors represented by the top two sections of Maslow's Pyramid are the factors that give us motive for action. The lower order needs, represented by the bottom three sections of the pyramid, don't move us to positive action when they are added, but they do reduce our motive for action when they are withheld or taken away.

It is the external factors that are the de-motivators and the internal factors that are the motivators. Think of it from a business standpoint for a moment. If you were to give an across the board raise, with money being an external factor, you would only get a temporary spike in productivity. It usually lasts one to two weeks. However, if you were to reduce pay for your company across the board, you would get a permanent reduction in productivity. On the other hand, if you were to follow a coaching model of success and recognize and praise specific behaviors of your people, then back it up with describing the behavior, how you felt about it, and the positive effect it had on you and/or the company, you would activate an internal pride that would yield greater motivation for that person.

Think about how a martial artist would react in class if you had been working with them for the last three weeks to perfect a front thrust kick. You have meticulously taught them about how to plant their foot, raise their knee, extend their leg and make contact with the ball of the foot as they thrust with their hip through the target. They have gotten it wrong fifty times and you have helped them understand their specific problem each time. Finally, they get it right! They knock the bag back 7 feet on the rail and you smile a big smile, then tell them how proud you are of them for remembering each step of the process and executing the kick perfectly. When you validate the specific action and result that they have gotten and back it up with positive emotion, it becomes a very easy choice for them to be motivated. That is the point that you have to get to. You have to understand how to position them to be internally driven for success. They will now work harder for you and will drive themselves to impress you even more because they now crave that feeling of accomplishment. This drive to "impress" you is the strongest when you consistently model the correct behaviors and actions for them. It is very difficult for them to describe, but they know they need to have it again. It is the positive emotional response that sets them on the path of working harder, doing their very best, practicing and focusing, and ultimately of succeeding. Always, look for and reward the things they are doing right!

As you begin to think about where you are in life and what you have accomplished, you begin to realize that you only do the things that you are motivated to do. This is, perhaps, the most important lesson in staying driven for success. Regardless of what is happening in your life or has happened to you, you can choose motivation. You can choose to take action, or have motive for success.

From Chip

When I was nine years old, I worked for my dad and could do virtually anything that he needed me to do in his shop. I could operate a fork-lift, a back-hoe, a

77

bull-dozer, or almost anything else that he needed. I remember one day when I was working in his shop and an employee of his, who was probably 19 years old, asked if I could take over the drill press while he went to the bathroom. I knew how to run it and didn't have any trouble stepping in where I was needed.

My father had told me earlier that day that I needed to replace my cotton gloves because they had become stringy and were coming apart. Most guys wanted to wear leather gloves, but my dad had always preferred cotton ones and I had followed that example. I had drilled a few holes, sweeping the metal shavings off the press each time and then pulling the next piece of metal up and pulling the press down. After a few holes had been drilled, I was sweeping away metal shavings from previous holes drilled and because I had not changed my gloves, and there were loose strings that could easily get caught in the bit, I ended up having my next significant accident. The drill bit caught those lose glove strings on the glove and continued to spin, it pulled my hand into the bit and drilled all the way through the center of my right hand.

I ended up having two surgeries on my right hand and was told at one point that they would have to take my thumb and replace it with one of my big toes. They said I likely would not ever regain full use of my hand because I had lost an entire muscle, and bunches of vascular and nervous tissue that had gotten wound up around the drill bit and yanked out of the hand. The future for my hand looked pretty bleak. But, due to the sheer determination of my mom and dad and months of recovery and physical therapy I did heal from the injury and kept my thumb. I was left with some trouble with writing (those that have seen my handwriting, might argue that I have more than "some trouble"). I do have numbness in the cold weather, and some loss of finger control due to the muscle loss. After that injury, just like after losing my eye, I had a choice to make. I could choose to let an injury define me or I could take action and put myself into motion for success. It wasn't always an easy choice, but it was always a choice. I was always able to choose the direction that I wanted to take for my life.

I had the kind of parents that made my choice much easier because they recognized the good things that I did instead of just the bad things. They believed in my ability to accomplish and helped me to believe as well. How many more kids today would go on to do incredible things if their parents, and coaches, and teachers openly believed in them and intentionally sought out the good things that they were doing? How many more adults today would make something incredible with their life if we taught them how to activate that motive for success that exists within them?

From Jody

I don't believe that we do anything that we are not motivated to do. I don't believe that we do homework in school unless we want to. I don't believe that we exercise unless we are motivated. I don't believe that we are successful unless we have that internal motive, or reasoning for success.

Athletic Outside of School

When I was in high school, I was athletic, but I was not a school athlete. I didn't play football, which in West Texas is the sport that seems to define athletics. I had played football in 8th grade, well, for one day in 8th grade. I ended my football career with a sweep to the left, carrying the ball, and getting crushed by a guy named Matt. I was a fairly small guy in 8th grade, but I had other circumstances that contributed.

Two and half weeks earlier, I had flipped a 3-wheeler and it had landed on the inside of my right thigh, causing a hairline fracture in my femur. I had been taken to the hospital in Amarillo to be checked out and was told to simply take it easy. I lived in Canadian, Tx at the time. "Take it easy" meant that I was not supposed to run, jump, kick, or play any contact sport for about six weeks. That was the note that the doctor had given us and that was the note that the coaches had received.

I hated being on the sidelines and wanted to be in the action, so I told the coach that I was good to play. He told me to go ahead and suit up then if I was good. From an accountability standpoint, I was at fault for going against what the doctor had instructed. The coach, who was the leader on the field, was also at fault for going directly against the instructions from my parents and the doctor.

When my leg broke, it shut down my athletics for the rest of the year. In fact, after being in traction in the hospital for almost a month, then in traction at home for another 12 weeks, and then in a regular cast for all but the last 2 weeks of my 8th grade year, I did no athletics that year. I had to decide whether or not to accept the negative things that the boys said about me that year, and the next. I had to decide whether or not I had the right motive for success moving forward.

Young people can be pretty mean in the things that they say. Even though the teasing about being crippled and the making fun of me for not playing football hurt, I decided to take action to be athletic. I simply chose to define myself instead of letting others define me. My athletic abilities were rooted in martial arts and gymnastics, both of which I did 6 days per week through the rest of high school. I even started lifting weights my sophomore year in order to make the sports that I loved better.

Don't Wait For Motivation To Show Up

I think that people wait too long for motivation to show up for them. I look at a lot of the guys that were athletic in high school and realize that most of them never mastered internal motivation. They never figured out how to drive themselves toward success. When you see the starting quarterback working the same job 15 years after high school that they had when they graduated, or the person with such potential to do something great with their abilities simply letting them go to waste, you realize that it isn't raw talent that matters the most. What truly matters is the ability to pick yourself up from an adversity and take action towards your next success. I don't regret the adversities that I have faced because they made me who I am today. I am driven to succeed because I know what it means to have to pick yourself back up and choose to move forward. The success formula that I have seen work time and time again in martial arts, as well as in corporate America, is fairly simple.

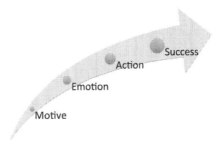

What is interesting about this formula is that it isn't actually a progressive one. It is a simultaneous implementation of the first three steps in order to achieve success. Your motive, emotion, and action all start at the exact same moment and each relies on the other two for sustainability. You must have a solid motive for what you desire to accomplish. Your motive must have an internal origin and be rooted in doing something good. Negative motives do push people towards action, but they also burn a person up. Negative motives, such as anger or hate, create negative and destructive emotions.

This leads to the second point, which is to have positive emotion tied to your success in the endeavor. You have to see the positive end results in your mind and those results have to make you feel better about yourself and life in general. If you don't have positive emotion tied to your direction, your motive won't stick.

The sustained action that is required of you will work when, and only when, your motive and your emotions are strong enough. Steven Pressfield, in his book <u>Do The Work</u>, said, "Amateurs wait for inspiration to show up before they take action. Professionals show and do the work." This is true of success in sales, leadership, martial arts, or anything else worthwhile that you do in life. Motive plus emotion plus action yields success.

If you get knocked down, learn from what didn't work and remember your motive, plus the positive emotion, and take action again. In an interview with Napoleon Hill, Thomas Edison said, "I had to create the incandescent light bulb. I knew that I would keep moving forward until I ran out of things that didn't work. If I had not already invented it, I would still be in my lab working instead of doing this interview." What if we had that same mentality about our success? What if we knew that we were going to keep coming back and working hard, trying new things, and shedding the old things? What if, as breakthrough leaders, we kept learning and growing until we were able to break through to our people and show them the way to succeed in life?

MOTIVATION QUOTE

"Motivation is the fuel, necessary to keep the human engine running." --Zig Ziglar

Lessons From the Masters

Your demonstration of personal motivation is the example that others have to follow.

Motivation is internally driven. De-Motivation is externally driven.

Motive, emotion, and action work in harmony to create success.

Being motivated is a choice that you make each and every day regardless of your circumstances.

YOUR BREAKTHROUGH!

Are you regularly demonstrating high levels of motivation?
If not, let's consider your why. Your why is what drives
you personally. Start here and write down your personal
why. What gets you out of bed, gets you fired up, makes
you want go?

_____

_____

_____

_____

_____

_____

_____

_____

_____

_____

_____

_____

_____

CHAPTER 7
C IS FOR COURTEOUS

Courtesy And the Lord's

servant must not be quarrelsome but kind to everyone, able to teach, patiently enduring evil, (2 Timothy 2:24 ESV)

"Life is not so short but that there is always time for courtesy." – Ralph Waldo Emerson

What an incredible thing it is to be courteous to those around us. It may seem ironic, since Tae Kwon Do is often perceived as violent, but courtesy is also commonly the first tenet of Tae Kwon Do taught. What a difference it makes when we treat each person with the respect and honor that they desire and deserve. We are all God's children, brothers and sisters no matter how you see it. Imagine a world where people are treated with the utmost respect, even if they have not "earned" it. Think about what life could be like if everyone was treated with respect, and extended the grace of common courtesy at all times to everyone.

Students of Tae Kwon Do learn that respecting others and being courteous to them is a part of the way in which they are supposed to live. It is intended to be an extension of themselves and representative of the way that they believe about the world. There is too much malice, too much self-centeredness in the world.

Drew Dudley, in a TED talk ® in Toronto talked about what he referred to as everyday leadership. This is the kind of leadership that makes a difference in each interaction that we have. Dudley said that we leave each person either better or worse as a result of each interaction that we have with them. So, leadership is really about the daily interactions that we have and living into the exact moment that we exist in.

Dudley went on to say that there really is NO reality.

There are only 5 billion or so versions/interpretations of reality. In each moment of your existence you are either making the world a better place or a worse place. This is based on what you believe, think, and act like in you daily interactions. The truth is that they were on to something with that "Golden Rule" thing. You know the one we are talking about…

Do unto others as you would have them do unto you.

"So whatever you wish that others would do to you, do also to them…" Matthew 7:12 ESV

"As" or "Before": BIG Difference

Most people try to do unto others *before* they do unto them. This attitude of pre-emptive vengeance will eat a person up. Focusing on what is wrong with others, or how you are going to get them before they get you will leave you an unhappy and unsatisfied person. In the next exercise, we want to test out what your gut or instinctual reactions are. This is your book. Write your answers honestly and see what the first thing to hit your brain is. Don't think about the questions. Answer them with the very first thing that comes to mind. You may be a little surprised by what is buried inside of you.

All politicians are: _____

Nurses always: _____

Blondes have: _____

Old people are: _____

Kids these days: _____

White people are: _____

Black people are: _____

Hispanics are: _____

Rich people are: _____

Poor people are: _____

The reality for most of us is that we have things that have been imprinted in our minds. It is that "imprinting" that continues to influence the way in which we treat others. It can be a little harsh to think about some of the things that were first to come to mind with the "First Thoughts" exercise that you just completed.

The good news for each of us is that what your first thoughts are is simply a result of conditioning and underlying beliefs. If you want to see the world in a new way, the simplistic key is to begin looking every day in every way for the positive that you are wanting. Whatever you go out of your way to look for, is what pops into your mind and ultimately into your life. Now, let's go through that exercise again, and this time, we want you to write down what you would like to think about each of the statements. Take some time to think through each one and fill in the blanks with the answer that represents the best you possible.

All politicians are: _____

Nurses always: _____

Blondes have: _____

Old people are: _____

Kids these days: _____

White people are: _____

Black people are: _____

Hispanics are: _____

Rich people are: _____

Poor people are: _____

You have to go out each and every day and make a concerted effort to find the good in the world. Being courteous to others requires that you look for the good that they have to offer. In the words of John Maxwell, "See everyone in life with a 10 on their forehead" and treat them like a ten in your life. It requires that you focus on the positives in the world and not just the negatives.

We have each had some great examples, as well as some not so great examples, of what it means to be courteous. Moreover, it's easy to fall into the "at least

I don't _____ " trap. You rationalize your actions with "at least I don't do" (Fill in the blank). Just remember, that not bad, isn't good, much less great. If, rather than being respectful and polite to others, you say to yourself, "well at least I don't", you are not being the leader you could be. Consider why courtesy is so important in John Maxwell's words, "People don't care how much you know until they know how much you care."

If you look back on your life, it is highly likely that someone in your family demonstrated to you what it meant to treat another person with respect. If not in your family, then look back in your memory to your teachers, coaches, or other leaders that have been a part of your life. If you still can't come up with the right example, that means something very important. It means that you are destined to be the right example for others in each of your interactions with them. It means that it is up to you to show others how amazing it can be to treat others with respect and courtesy. Initiate every interaction with others with utmost courtesy and respect.

Be Proper, Rise Above

"Courtesy is as much a mark of a gentleman as courage." – Theodore Roosevelt

It is interesting to look at the origin and meaning of the word courteous. The word first came into use in the mid 14th Century. It originally meant "having courtly manners." Being a part of the courts was reserved for those who understood the proper ways in which to behave with others. It meant that you were supposedly more intelligent and more educated than the common man. It represented someone who was both genteel and kind in the way they interacted with others. To be a courteous person meant that you were not in the same league with the rest of the world. It meant that you had risen above the normality of life and had become a part of the elite who understood the value of people and the value of treating others in a respectful and mannered way. If you have ever looked at this world and wondered why people didn't have better manners, then you have wondered why others did not embrace the idea of courtesy. How many examples do young people still have of others being truly courteous? How many young people understand chivalry because they have witnessed it happening all around them? We haven't thought of enough examples either. That is why the teaching of courtesy is so important. It is why leaders within companies so desperately need to treat their supervisors, coworkers, and especially their employees with courtesy. It is us to you, as a leader, to break through the social norms of today and initiate a positive change. It is critical that you make it your focus to leave each person better than you found them through courteous and professional interactions.

From Chip

When I was a young boy, I watched the respect that my father had for my mother. I watched how he would hold doors for her, go out of his way to show her that he cared, and demonstrated courtesy when they interacted. It wasn't just my mother that received courtesy, though. I was able to see him, as well as my mom, treat others with courtesy, even if they had not earned their respect. Several times, I even witnessed them being polite when it was obvious that the other people did not deserve the kind treatment.

The misconception that a lot of people have about martial arts is that it is about fighting. While it is definitely true that a student can become a master at defending, and even attacking, but the underlying philosophy of martial arts is one of harmony. Students learn the arts in order to first master themselves and then to master the circumstances of the world around them. It really is about learning to see the best in the world instead of the worst. It's about finding the golden nugget in the "mud" that you are in at the moment. A line from Karen Eden's poem, "I am a Martial Artist" says it this way; "Though trained for bodily harm my intentions are for peace."

It's always awesome to see the diverse students of martial arts on the mat next to each other showing each other great courtesy, respect and camaraderie no matter their back grounds, education levels, jobs… Commonly, in one class, we might have an eye surgeon right next to a young person who busses tables, next to a school teacher, next an academic student, next to an attorney, and they all treat each other with great mutual respect. The instructors model this. Each student is valued and appreciated. The power of common courtesy goes a long way when you want to influence or lead people.

I think back to that teacher I had in the second grade. My life could have been dramatically different. For me, those not at all polite words lit a fire. But what did they do to others? I probably won't ever know, but that experience impacted me in a huge way.

Finally, the lyrics from Hawk Nelson's song, "Words", say a lot about the power of being polite and courteous as we interact with those we lead:
> "Words can build you up
> Words can break you down
> Start a fire in your heart
> Or Put it out.
> Let my words be life
> Let my words be truth
> I don't wanna say a word
> Unless it points the world back to You."

From Jody

I was blessed to grow up with some great examples of leadership and courtesy in my life. From a very early age, I witnessed people treating others with respect. What always stood out for me were the times that I saw people being mean to another person and the other person simply seeing the good in them.

I remember looking at the "nice" people and thinking about how much I wanted to be remembered as that nice person instead of the mean one. I believe that being able to witness both courtesy and discourtesy demonstrated which path was right for me. I believe that I was able to choose the direction that I wanted for my life because I never wanted to be that person who hurt others. I wanted to be the person that lifted others up by treating them with the utmost respect and honor.

I loved reading about Ghandi when I was younger. The things that he accomplished through non-violence and courteous interaction were incredible. He was able to interact with the British and demonstrate to all of India that battles can be won without a physical fight. My belief is that we abandon courtesy when we are consumed with fear, particularly fear of our version of reality not staying in tact.

COURTESY QUOTE

"Nothing is ever lost by courtesy. It is the cheapest of pleasures, costs nothing, and conveys much. It pleases him who gives and receives and thus, like mercy, is twice blessed." - Erastus Wiman

Lessons From the Masters

All life deserves respect.

Don't judge a book by its cover. Don't stereotype based on looks, initial actions, possessions, or any other superficial factors.

Don't react poorly in heated moments, wait 24 hours and respond intelligently, with courtesy.

We tend to be mirrors reflecting what we receive. Give courtesy first, and you will be much more likely to receive it in return.

Additionally, leaders who understand the concept of "Do it because you can", receive BUY IN from their teams.

Leaders who expect "Do it because I said so", receive resistance.

YOUR BREAKTHROUGH!

Can you think of times that you walked past someone and had the opportunity to speak politely, but did not do so? Later you find out that the person is the parent of a good friend, and you get a small but deep feeling of regret in your belly that you did not initiate a kind gesture. Well, ponder that for a moment, and learn.

We all feel so much better when we do not have that regretful feeling over missing something that seems so simple! You know, and we do too.

So we challenge you for the next 21 days to be the initiator of a kind gesture at every opportunity that presents itself. For example, when you have that little feeling rise up that you should wave at the neighbor in their yard…DO IT FIRST. Be the one that everyone wants to be around, because you are always, always so courteous. Take a moment and write out at least three ways that you can demonstrate courtesy on a daily basis and let this be your guide to being a more courteous you.

_____

_____

_____

_____

_____

CHAPTER 8
H IS FOR HONEST

H _Honesty_ _Better is a poor person who walks in his integrity than one who is crooked in speech and is a fool. (Proverbs 19:1 ESV)_

"It is better to offer no excuse than a bad one."
--George Washington

Being honest with yourself can be one of the most difficult things that you ever do. The world often tells us that it is okay to "bend" the truth in order to fit our needs at that moment. From an ethics standpoint, the world has adjusted its perception of reality. This isn't necessarily a good thing. We have seen the concept of being "honest" go from an absolute to a legalistic to a situational to a rational viewpoint. The four different views of what it means to be honest have left a lot of young people wondering where they find the right example of what to do as they grow up.

Take a look around at the superstars of the day. How many celebrities do we see that do things that are illegal and then turn around and "lawyer up" to get out of the responsibility of the situation? How many times have we seen examples of people who admit, and then retract their responsibility for something that they did? Because being an example is such an integral part of the Team Chip philosophy, it is imperative that people learn what it means to operate with honesty in everything that they do and that starts with being honest with yourself.

Being completely honest isn't easy. It is perhaps th most difficult for us to be completely honest with ourselves. This is much tougher than deciding to be honest with those around us. You can most likely think back to certain times in your life where you were faced with a harsh reality of who you had demonstrated yourself to be. You may not have liked the person that you saw in the mirror when you thought about the negative actions or bad behaviors you had exhibited. Many times, we react out of emotion instead of acting out of love because we have not taken the 24 hour rule seriously. This is the rule that says you need to take 24 hours to cool off before responding when you are upset. That cooling off period gives you time to gain perspective and think through what you are going to say. It is important to be both honest and courteous in your responses.

If you pretend that what you are doing that is wrong it isn't so bad or you rationalize that others are worse than you, you might not change. You might not become the person you could be because making up excuses about our own behavior is still an act of dishonesty. When you have make up excuses as to why you didn't do what you were supposed to do, you give up a piece of yourself. You are saying that you don't respect yourself enough to be fully honest in that situation.

Fully Honest

Being a martial artist, just like being a leader, means that you are commonly held to a higher standard than the world around you. As a matter of fact, the rank structure and earning environment of martial arts makes most, not all, experienced martial artists...leaders. This standard will push you, challenge you, and test your ethical viewpoint on a regular basis. Those who are fully honest with themselves will know when they need an accountability partner because they can't be trusted to succeed honestly on their own. Those who are fully honest with themselves will proactively seek out accountability partners and mentors. Those who are fully honest with themselves will strive to succeed at every turn. Let's take a look at the four levels of ethics. Identify which level you believe you are living at and then identify which level you are.

Absolute Ethics – Absolute ethics could be defined as an absolute right and an absolute wrong. This would mean that there are no circumstances or conditions that would dictate an interpretation of a behavior. Each act that a person performs is either right or wrong, regardless of the situation that they are in. For example, if stealing is wrong, then stealing is wrong. You might ask, "But what if I was stealing to feed my family?" With absolute ethics, stealing to feed your family is just as wrong as stealing for fun. If killing another person is wrong, then it would not matter if the person was attacking you, killing them would be wrong. You would have to go back a very, very long time to find people that operated with absolute ethics in every aspect of their lives. There are certain things in almost every person's life that are absolutes to them. You may feel absolute about taking the Lord's name in vain to be wrong, no matter what. You may feel absolute about cheating on tests. What is interesting is that most people will have a few absolutes in their life, even though most of what they believe falls into one of the other three categories of ethics. The next level down in ethical thought is the legalistic view of ethics.

Legalistic Ethics – The person who believes in a

legalistic viewpoint of ethics sees the world based on a set of accepted rules. It is interesting to see the rules change and then see the new vantage point of the legalist. The legalistic ethics viewpoint would see that running a red light is illegal and wrong. If you were in the downtown area of a town of about 80,000 people and there wasn't anyone around. You were the only one at the light, the legalist would not run the light. They would look at the rule and determine what the law, or accepted structure of the area, would say about it. With the example of killing, the legalist would believe that killing is wrong, unless they are justified in defending themselves with deadly force. The difficult part for the legalist is the change in rules that can happen, or the reinterpretation of law. As the rules change, they struggle to accept new norms or standards. Many of the people who believe in legalistic ethics are drawn to work in the area of enforcing the legal structure of the law. The third level of ethics is that of situational ethics.

Situational Ethics – The person who believes in situational ethics is always measuring behaviors against the circumstances of the moment. They look at the idea of telling a lie and measure the cost/benefit ratio in their mind. If telling the lie can be justified for the given situation, then they tell the lie. They look at behaviors like stealing and determine whether or not the stealing can be justified against the situation that they are in. They would see that stealing really isn't wrong if it means that they are preventing their family from starving. Every ethical choice is based on the circumstances that they find themselves in. This is much tougher on the person making the choices because they really don't have a solid set of rules to fall back on for making their choices. They will often look at the legalistic view and determine how bad their choice is and if they can get around the letter of the law. They rely on the spirit of the law instead of the rule of law. The fourth type of ethics is that of rational ethics.

Rational Ethics – This is a very open view of right and wrong. The person who operates with rational ethics will say things like, "As long as I am not hurting anyone else, what does it matter." They view their choices in the world as good as long as they feel that their intentions are good. Rational ethics allows for an adjustment of standards based on emotional response. This means that this person might steal from a store or a company and feel perfectly fine about it as long as the store has insurance and will get reimbursed. They will say that "nobody got hurt." This is the most self-driven view of ethics. It is the one that often leads to people taking larger and larger steps away from the rules. Many people who operate with rational ethics will end up crossing the line legally and will put themselves in bad situations. Honesty is simply an interpretation for the person who operates with rational ethics.

People often look at the idea of being completely honest and believe that this action would make them mean. The first question that most men ask us is, "What if my wife asks if she looks overweight and I think that she does?" They want to know if it is okay to lie in that situation. They are wanting a "legal opinion" of a situation that they believe could be easily rationalized. Being honest isn't always easy. In fact, we would argue that being honest is much tougher than simply doing what you want in any situation or rationalizing your behaviors away. Being easier definitely does not mean that it is right, though.

Don't Compromise

There are three key areas that we see honesty as an absolute. If you believe that you are a leader and you desire to break through barriers with your teams, then these three areas cannot be compromised. You will have to look inside of yourself and decide if you want to be an honest person. The three areas that are critical are:

1. Honesty with yourself
2. Honesty with your teams
3. Honesty with those that you serve as an example for

Start With You

We've all met the "pot that calls the kettle black" person. They're the person that's great at pointing out everything that needs to be changed beyond their nose, but fail to see, the "log in [their] own eye". See Matthew 7:5.

Being honest with yourself is the one that gets most people. It is a challenge, but not impossible to be honest with other people about their shortcomings.

It is even easy to be honest with others about what they are good at. It is another thing, entirely, to be honest with ourselves about who we are and where we are.

You have to be willing to be introspective and identify what you struggle with and what you are good at. Your struggles, when you hit them the right way, can help to build you into the best person possible. When you are struggling, you must be willing to let someone know that you need help, find a guide, mentor and/or an accountability partner. You must be willing to put yourself out there and admit your weakness. If you have built a trusting team, then this level of honesty and vulnerability will make your leadership even stronger. When you are gifted in an area, you must be willing to accept that you have something to offer the world. By offering your gifts to the world, you help to fulfill the purpose for which you were created.

Tact With Your Teams

Being honest with your teams means that you are tactfully direct in your leadership and communication. Tact is defined as the non-abrasive communication of important and/or sensitive information. Being direct can lead to you saying things in a mean-spirited or demeaning manner if you are not careful. Your job is to communicate with your team, your students, your coworkers in such a way that they get the importance of the message without putting up communication roadblocks. Being mean spirited or even perceived as mean spirited is definitely a road block to good communication.

Your messaging leads to their response, so be aware of how you come across. You have to be honest with your teams about where they are, where you need them to be, and the expectation of their success.

Set up to Fail

The world often hides the truth of how a person is doing at work and even in martial arts. People are promoted even though they don't have the requisite skills to be at that next level. William J. Peters coined the term, "The Peter Principle" to describe the promotion of a person beyond their capabilities. When a person is promoted beyond what they are prepared for, they are being set up for failure. When a supervisor tells an employee that they are doing just fine on a performance review, yet the employee is failing, then that employee will not realize what they need to work on.

Several years ago, it was a common for military men and women stationed overseas to be put through an "accelerated" martial arts program. Because Abilene, TX is also home to an Air Force Base, periodically a "black belt" who went through one of these programs would come to us to continue their training.

One time in particular was quite memorable, and honestly really sad. Because of the rank structure, the "black belt" (I use quotes not to make fun of him, but to make a distinction) lined up at the head of the class.

After just a few minutes, it was apparent that the accelerated program was not up to par. Green belts in our academy (at least seven belts below the black belt) were kicking higher, faster, harder, and with better technique. The "black belt" saw it, as did people watching.

Honesty says that there isn't a fast track or a bypass. Being honest, we take the long way around. I'm not sure if it was contentment, embarrassment, or frustration, but that "black belt" came to three or four classes, and then never returned.

Promoting someone beyond their level or skill or competency can break someone's spirit quicker than holding them until the right time ever will.

Our job as breakthrough leaders is to honestly prepare our teams for success. If we hide the struggles that a person is having and hope they will simply quit soon, then we are not setting an example of an honest leader. We are the example that others will follow. This means that your level of honesty with and about yourself, as well as your level of honesty with your teams will strongly influence their behaviors.

Be an Example

The third area of required honesty is to serve as an example for those that look to you as an example. Here is the kicker: you are an example for every person that you meet. Every encounter that you have with another person will leave them either better off or worse off. The example that you set in every interaction that you have every day of your life is important. You are the example that others look to. In an August 19, 2011 blog post on teamchiptkd.com, the definition of a black belt was given. That blog showed that being a black belt went well beyond self defense, kicking, and punching. Being a black belt is about living your life in the right manner so that others will follow the right example. John Maxwell, in his book 21 Irrefutable Laws of Leadership, said, "If you think you are a leader and you find that no one is following, then you're just out taking a walk."

I don't believe that you are simply taking a walk through this life. People who seek out ways to become breakthrough leaders are the ones that are on the path to build a better world. It is your example in every action, in every reaction, in every interaction that you have that will build the world around you. Never forget that others are watching. Your honesty and your example are what this world needs.

From Chip

When I'm teaching Tae Kwon Do at Team Chip we regularly execute what we call mat chats. These mat chat are vital for several reasons:

1. They allow us as leaders to communicate very important character building information like the tenets of Tae Kwon Do (Courtesy, Integrity, Perseverance, Self-Control…)to our students while we have their undivided

attention.

2. They allow us to address important matters from outside the Tae Kwon Do school to the students. For example if a student had a rough day at work or school today due to failing at a task, we get an opportunity to encourage all the students to learn from their poor performance and grow, and never give up in a blanket conversation that does not single out or embarrass any one person. This allows everyone to benefit from this learning experience together.

3. Mat chats allow us to communicate important information to the parents in attendance when teaching younger students.

4. They allow us to refocus the students, by changing the pace of a class.

Many times in these mat chats, one of my favorite topics is honesty. I will pick a student and say let's pretend that you are going to hold my favorite cupcake for a minute. I need to leave the room, and will be right back. Will you do it, please? The student always says "yes sir" and the lesson begins.

I pretend to leave and come back in and see that my cupcake is missing!! I will ask the student, "Where is my cupcake?" and they usually respond with, "I do not know, sir." I will then ask, "Did you eat my cupcake?" They will say "no sir." I will say, "Are you sure you didn't eat it?" They will again say "no sir!" I will ask, "Where is my cupcake?" They usually say something like, "I don't know or I didn't eat it, sir." I will then say, "Ok, but I see crumbs on your shirt and icing on your lips!! I think you ate my cupcake!" They will all smile and respond with uuuhhh ooohh!!! I will then ask them this question, "How many lies did you tell me about the cupcake in this situation?" They all typically have to ponder this for a minute. I will then explain that by initially telling me that they did not know where my cupcake went, that they had told lie number one. Then when I asked if they ate it, they had to tell lie number two to cover lie number one. I work to get them to see that telling one lie, leads to telling another and another, and another many times with the intent of covering the first lie. Then I ask them if they really think I would be upset if they ate my cupcake and they know that I would not. I tell them if you ate my cupcake and admitted to me, "I was hungry and ate it, sir", it would be difficult for me to really be upset, it was just a simple cupcake and they were hungry. BUT, since they lied about the cupcake's disappearance, which then lead to a lie about eating it, now I'm twice as upset, because they told me two lies to cover the fact that thy ate the cupcake without permission to begin with!

In this example, I stress that taking ownership of eating the cupcake without permission in the beginning, would be a much better option than being dishonest about eating it and causing them to bury themselves in lies. The goal here is teaching them that what appears as one simple lie leads to more and more lies, and potentially a life of dishonesty. A life of dishonesty leads to a life of poor relationships, because no one can trust you, if you fail to take ownership of your actions, and fail to be an honest person.

From Jody

I grew up as the son of a Methodist Preacher. I remember my father talking to me regularly about the example that I set by the things that I said and the things that I did. He spent several of those key conversations discussing what it meant to be honest. In hindsight, I find it a little frustrating that he had to explain to me what honesty was. We have complicated our world to the point that it is not a simple answer any more. In the ethics course that I teach for companies, I ask them a very simple question…

"Is it wrong to tell a lie?"

Most people will say that it is definitely wrong to tell a lie. I then ask the married men in the room a different question. I tell them to think about when their wife was getting ready to go out to dinner with them and they asked the question, "Do these pants make my butt look big?" I have always gotten a resounding response that it is okay to lie in that situation. Some men say that they are telling a lie for self-preservation. Others say that they are telling a lie because it would be mean to be honest in that situation.

The place that we seem to find ourselves in society is that people often view honesty as a situational choice. I have even found that people will help you lie because the lie is less painful. I was late to a meeting early on in business, because I had not put it on my calendar. The person that I was to meet with had called me on my cell phone to check on me. When I answered the phone they said, "I just wanted to check on you. I am sure something happened that prevented you from being at the meeting with me 20 minutes ago." I had a choice to make in that situation. I could go with the lie that was offered to me or I could be honest. I am thankful that I had been taught in both my family and in my martial arts to be honest. I responded with, "I would like to make up an excuse, but the truth is that I did not plan well and I didn't even put the meeting on my calendar. It is completely my fault." There was silence on the other end of the line for a while, and then laughter. She asked me, "Do you think that you could teach my staff that?" I asked, "You mean to be late or to be honest?" She said, "To be honest. When can we get together to discuss how you could do that?" I told her that I didn't have anything right then, which made her chuckle again, and I headed to her office. The lesson that I learned is that being honest isn't always easy but it is the right thing to do.

HONESTY QUOTE

"Honesty is the first chapter of the book wisdom."
  --Thomas Jefferson

"You can fool some of the people all of the time, and all of the people some of the time, but you cannot fool all of the people all of the time."
  --Abraham Lincoln

Lessons From the Masters

Honesty with yourself is many times very difficult, yet foundational to being honest with others.

Honesty needs to be a habit in your life.

Honesty is the foundation of trust.

Trust is the foundation of relationships.

YOUR BREAKTHROUGH!

It's time to make a decision to be your best. You must truly look deep inside and see who you really are.

Schedule a time with a trusted friend or family member and sit with them. It needs to be someone that knows you WELL and that you TRUST deeply. It should be someone that you feel will not take advantage of your vulnerability, but will be very honest with you. Ask them to be completely transparent with you, and share with you what they see from their perspective about you. Have them share the strengths they perceive. Then, ask for the things they perceive as needing improvement. THIS can be very difficult, because people will often want to "defend" their perceived weaknesses. That's ok, it is normal to feel that way! Just don't defend them! Accept them and learn from them.

I will meet with (person's name) _____
_____ to discuss my strengths and weaknesses. We will
get together on the day and time below and I will
write out the strengths and weaknesses that they share
with me.

Date and Time: _____

Have a list of questions for them and ask them to rate
you on a scale of 1-10 (1=low ; 10=highest):

"How do you see my integrity?" _____

"How do you see my work ethic?" _____

"How is my communication skill / ability?"_____

"Am I a team player?" _____

"Am I personable/friendly?" _____

Ask some open ended questions also:
"Have I ever let you down and how?"

_____

_____

"If I did let you down, did I apologize and repair the
damage, or do I need to do a better repair job? What
would you have liked to see from me?"

_____

"If you could change anything about me, what would it be?"

These questions are important, because what they perceive from you, most others will perceive from you as well.

As you can see, this exercise will be tough. You will need to be ready to be patient, open minded, ready to learn, and more. You will need to remember that you are asking for the feedback so you can grow. LET THEM FINISH THEIR SENTENCES WITH OUT INTERRUPTING.

Remember to thank them for their time and help!!!! Now get ready to get to work on the feedback.

Live as an honest example of great leadership!

CHAPTER 9
I IS FOR INSPIRED

I *Inspiration* _Show yourself in

all respects to be a model of good works,
and in your teaching show integrity,
dignity, (Titus 2:7 ESV)

"Perpetual optimism is a force multiplier."
Colin Powell

Looking at the origin of the word "inspire" opens up an understanding of what we, as breakthrough leaders, are called to do every day in our lives. The word inspire, according to it etymology (origin) traces back to the 13th century. The Latin version of the word was described as the process of enflaming, or building a fire within. The French used a variation of the word to describe the process of inducing, or drawing out from another person, greatness. The Greek version of the word meant to animate with an idea or purpose. No matter which translation of the word that you identify with most, the reality is that when we inspire others, it is our objective to draw the very best out of them. Our job as leaders is to help people see the potential that exists within themselves.

From Chip

I think about the life that my mom described that I would live a lot. I remember hearing over and over again, from her, that I would be the kind of man that others wanted to be like. I have no doubt that I didn't really understand what she meant when I was young. I just knew that I was supposed to raise my standards. No matter where I was at in life, the expectation from my parents was that I lived with higher standards for myself and for the people that I associated with. At 3 years old, there was no way for me to fully grasp the principle of inspiring others. As an adult, though, I have come to grasp a better understanding of the importance of living above the mediocrity.

I want you think about the interactions that you have in every area of your life. Whether it is face to face or in your social media, you are responsible for the example that you set. A part of your remaining an inspired and inspiring leader is to watch what you say, post, like, or comment on. When you lower your standards and allow the negativity of others create a response in you, then you are giving over control to others. You are giving up your standards of who you know you were meant to be and letting someone else's standards take over. Like Lilly Tomlin once said, "The problem with the rat race is that only rats run it." You can't expect to remain an inspiring leader if you are lowering your standards to negatively interact with someone whose goal it is to bring people down, in essence trying to bring themselves up.

If you are on the job, at school, or in the gym, when someone is working to bring a person down, your job is to bring them back up. This can be done by direct intervention or indirectly by saying and doing things to counteract the negativity of the person. Some of the greatest instructors that I have ever known were the ones that simply refused to believe that people couldn't achieve greatness. Some of the greatest social media influencers that I have known are the ones who understand when it is time to go radio silent. This is a term that I encourage my students with in reference to not responding on social media. Going radio silent is necessary when a person is making negative or disparaging comments about you, or pretty much anything else for that matter. You simply refrain from lowering your standards and jumping in there. You keep your self out of the mess. To some this may appear weak, but it takes great self-control, and allows for the 24 hour rule to be engaged. Not reacting, but intelligently responding correctly if necessary. I regularly remind our people that it is easy to be aggressive, be mean, flex your ego…from behind the safety of your key board in your pajamas in your cozy home. Remember to ask yourself, "Would I say this or act this way in person?" If not, cool down and think it through.

Crabs in the Basket

I am sure that you have seen the people who have a tendency to "stir the pot" to make things worse or to try and get people upset about something. These folks are the "Crabs in the basket", always trying to nay-say your dreams, plans, goals. They are many times so uncomfortable with growth that they make efforts to keep you from growing. These people thrive on bringing other people down to their level, they are the opposite of inspirational.

They feel better about themselves when others feel bad, just like them. One of the key lessons in martial arts, and one that my mom understood when I was 3, is that we are to live our lives above the mess. I was taught that if someone knocks me into a mud puddle to sit up! Sitting up gets you half way out of the problem immediately, as opposed to wallowing in the problem like a pig. If you are going to be a part of stirring the "poop" pot, you are putting yourself in the pot. That isn't where you were designed to be. You were designed to be above that mess!

When I joined martial arts, after years of doctors and coaches telling me I would have no depth perception, my hand injury would limit my ability to play ball sports and that I would have to be a "desk" worker in my future, that I was too tall to be fast, too tall to be flexible... I was unknowingly hungry for inspiration. Through many trials and tribulations, martial arts became a big part of that inspiration. My parents had always believed in me and believed that I could accomplish anything that I was willing to work for. I was inspired by them to continue trying to push myself and believe in myself. Once I was in martial arts, I began really seeing the potential that was always inside of me.

Because of my being inspired by martial arts, I often wonder how many people in this world are simply waiting for the right inspiration to release their greatness. I wonder how many more incredible leaders we would have if each person became inspired, motivated, and believed that a big part of their life was supposed to be dedicated to inspiring greatness in others. What would happen for you today if you made it a point to inspire someone? What would happen in your life today if you were inspired by someone? You will leave every person different than you found them. Leave them inspired to greatness!

From Jody

Every interaction that we have with another person will leave them either better or worse. It never leaves them the same as they are right now. An inspiring leader is one that understands that their job is to lift people up and make them into a better person than they could have been on their own. You are always inspiring someone to be something or do something. You may be inspiring them to greatness or you may be inspiring them to lower their standards. To "induce action" in a certain direction means that you are pulling people some place that they would not have gone without you. What is scary about this is that you are, even unknowingly, continuously changing the lives of other people as they model your behaviors.

Inspired By Terry

I have often thought back to Jr. High School, when I was a scrawny little kid and the bigger boys used to pick on me. I am sure that, in their mind, they were just having fun. In my mind, it wasn't that way, though. In my mind, they were doing their best to bring me down to their level of behavior. They were trying to get me to feel bad so that they would feel better. Whatever their actual intent was, the end result was me learning how to deal with the situation in such a way that it would change the course of my future actions. There was one kid, Terry Harrington, that really surprised me. He had moved to my town from another small Texas town and had experienced some rough times growing up. I don't know if he saw me like a little brother or felt sorry for me or just didn't want to see other people hurt. Whatever the case was, he went out of his way to step in several times when I was being picked on. One of the guys who liked to pick on anyone that he saw as a target was giving me a hard time and Terry stepped between me and that other kid. He told the guy that if he ever picked on me again, he would be messing with Terry as well. That was the first time that I remember being inspired by someone my own age. Terry stepped in a couple more times that year for me. By the third time, people understood that he was serious about being there for me. A couple of other guys followed Terry's example and began standing up for me when one of the bullies tried something. What really amazed me was that those other guys, who began standing up for me, would never have done that without the example that Terry set. It made me begin thinking about the example that I was setting and how it influenced others.

This really did change the course of my future. When I was a freshman in high school, I grew a lot. I grew almost a foot in 14 months. I got bigger, stronger, faster, and tougher. Guys have the false illusion of invincibility when they are bigger than other guys. By my Junior year in high school, I was in shape, lifting weights, and doing kick-boxing. I want you to think back to my story from the very beginning of this book. Defending my friend came from my experience with Terry.

Not Cool

There was a kid that, physically, was way behind what the rest of the class was. I had moved off to another town at the end of my sophomore year and was with all new people. I was never the "kid who got picked on" in the new school. I remember that I had worked really hard on developing a strong grip and could match grip with almost anyone around me. On several occasions, I shook this smaller kid's hand and put him to his knees. I am not at all proud of that behavior. It was probably the third or fourth time that I was going to do this that an image of Terry standing up for me popped into my head and I stopped in the middle of the handshake. I looked at the guy and I apologized for my stupid behavior. I told him that I would never do that again. I also told him that I would step in if anyone ever tried to do that, or any other bullying to him. Little did I know that the very next day would give me that opportunity.

My Turn

I was at a football game when two guys, who were bigger than him, were pushing him around and laughing at how easy it was to shove him. I stepped physically in the middle of them and put on my "fight face" to get their attention. Most black belts know what face that is. It is the open eyes, ears pulled back, jaw forward, and adrenaline pumping, kind of face. I also crossed my arms to try and make my arms appear bigger than they were. I let them know that this guy was my friend and that they would never mess with him again without messing with me. They got the message and apologized. I don't know if my actions meant as much to him as Terry's did to me, but I do know that we have to start somewhere in changing the minds and hearts of others. We have to inspire others to make better choices. What are you doing on a daily basis to inspire others?

INSPRIATION QUOTES

"Leadership is action, NOT position." Unknown

"You are what you do, not what you say you'll do."
--C.G. Jung

Lessons From the Masters

In Team Chip TKD, we strive to live our lives at the highest standards. We are working hard to create and maintain an environment of growth, an environment where expectations are clear and high, an environment where you are not ridiculed for falling, but pulled back up and encouraged for your willingness to step out and fall.

It is unfortunate when people leave the environment where they are pushed daily to raise their standards and join an environment where they are already the best. The reason that this is unfortunate is that when you start hanging around people that don't push you to your highest level, then you lose that intensity that comes with striving to always match or beat the next level up personally. When you train with people that are as good or better than you, you tend to work harder. You become inspired by the strength of those around you. In business, when you compete against the best, you move up faster. You realize that you have to put in significantly more effort to win. It is the intensity of your focus on being inspired and inspiring that will create the results that you have in life. Never back down on that intensity!

Surround yourself with people who live as the ideal versions of themselves and continue to work hard to grow daily. Remember that it is said that we become the average of the five people we spend the most time with. Who are you surrounding yourself with daily?

You see, in any situation, you can evaluate where you are at and what your ideal you is, based on a simple formula.

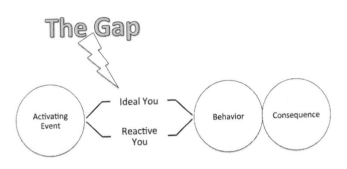

These are the ABC's of choosing to live an inspired life. You have to look at any activating event and weigh your options for the behavior that you will choose to exhibit. In that moment, if you have conditioned yourself to be an inspiration to others, it is much easier to choose to be the ideal you, the inspirational you, versus the reactive you, the un-inspirational you. Once an event or situation arises, if you already know that inspiring others is an integral part of how you will live, you will seek out ways to be the ideal version of yourself.

Just Get Mad? If You Want to be a Puppet

You could think about how a person acts in the sparring ring to really understand the gap. Parents will often yell at their kid to "get mad" when they are sparring, particularly when they are at a tournament. That is literally the worst thing that a fighter could do. They shouldn't get mad. They should stay in control. As soon as the other person is pulling the strings on your emotions in the ring, they own you. You have just given up control in "the gap." You have handed over the steering wheel of your mind to that person and you are at their mercy.

When you lose control of your emotions, you lose control of you. When you take this lesson outside of the ring into life, it doesn't change. If you are in a boardroom discussion and someone tries to provoke you, you have a choice to make about who you are. If you have pre-decided that you will be the one that maintains control of your emotions, then you will stay in control of you. You will be able to be the ideal version of yourself. If you have not pre-decided to live an inspired and in-control life, then you will very likely be at the mercy of the other person. They will be able to "pull your strings" and take you any direction that they want. Don't participate in the bullying, manipulation, name-calling, or negativity that happens at every age. This isn't something that only happens in Junior High. If you don't believe us, get on Facebook (social media) and watch the comments that people make about other people. Be the best version of you that you can be.

Your power to inspire resides within the gap between the activating event and the behavior that you choose. This is a decision that you have to make before you get into the situation, though. You have to decide how you intend to live your life. Never forget that every behavior that you exhibit will have a consequence. The consequence will either be a good one because you lived as the ideal you (you take time to respond well), or it will be a bad one because you simply reacted (you allowed emotions to control you). It takes only a single decision to change the course of your own life. Just as important, it takes only a single act of inspired living to change the course of another person's life. Choose not to lower your standards and participate in the reactive life. Choose to raise your standards and demonstrate an inspired life!

What we would like for you to do is to describe five things that you can do on a daily basis to leave others inspired to be more than they have been in the past.

YOUR BREAKTHROUGH!

Today, I will do these five things in order to raise my standards and leave others focused on the possibilities of who they can be. I will demonstrate these five things in order to keep my standards as high as possible and inspire others to the greatness that they were intended to accomplish.

1. _____

2. _____

3. _____

4. _____

5. _____

When you take action on a daily basis to leave others inspired, you will find that you live as the ideal you. You will also find that living this intentional, inspired life by encouraging, helping, motivating, and inspiring others, you'll have a breakthrough to your best life! Regardless of the activating event, your behaviors lead to positive consequences for you and for others when you are the person that you could be. Go out and inspire others to greatness today!

CHAPTER 10
P IS FOR PERSERVERING

P _Perseverance_ But they who wait for the Lord shall renew their strength; they shall mount up with wings like eagles; they shall run and not be weary; they shall walk and not faint. (Isaiah 40:31 ESV)

"Nothing in the world can take the place of persistence. Talent will not; nothing is more common than unsuccessful men with talent. Genius will not; unrewarded genius is almost a proverb. Education will not; the world is full of educated derelicts. Persistence and determination alone are omnipotent. The slogan

Press On! has solved and always will solve the problems of the human race."

--Calvin Coolidge

The influences that you have in your life do make a tremendous difference. On a person's journey to black belt, one of the primary objectives is to see whether or not they have the tenacity, veracity and intensity to keep on going. Getting back up one more time can be an extremely difficult feat. When a person starts out in martial arts, they learn to fall down. They learn to fall in such a way that it doesn't keep them down. As they move up through the ranks, their ability to remain persistent or their willingness to give up becomes clear.

The truth is, struggles reveal our true selves; the tests can become testimony. We can get up, or give in. What story do you want to tell?

To us, persevering is not simply a discipline thing. Persevering is a way in which we would describe ourselves. Each of us will have problems in our lives. Each of us will struggle and go through trials. It is the struggle that reveals who we are. The struggle doesn't make us. It chips away the rough edges to show the person that we are beneath the surface. The challenges that we face purify us as leaders. Max Lucado, in his book On The Anvil, outlines the reasoning for the struggles that we face. By being pushed into the fire and pounded on, we become the leaders that we were always intended to be.

Too many times, in this life, people run from the trials and tribulations that come their way. They do their best to stay sheltered from the harsh realities of life. They shelter their kids from struggles and sometimes even from hard work. When successful people have discussed with us what got them to the place they are at, they commonly talk about the tough times that they faced more than they talk about the successes.

The bigger the struggle you face, the bigger the victory you achieve. If you have problems, be thankful. This means that you're moving forward. This means that you are out there taking a risk. Martial arts is one of the best ways to teach people to persevere. More than the fact that you are training your body, you're training your spirit and your mind. Your teaching yourself that you can achieve more than your body or mind believes. Once you have achieved success in martial arts, you know that you can achieve success in any other area of life. You know that you are prepared.

From Chip

I have had my fair share of struggles throughout my life. People have even asked me why I was not bitter. Whether it was losing an eye at three years old or drilling through my hand at nine years old, or severing my Achilles as an adult, I simply chose not to let the circumstances control who I was. I believe that people who live with this breakthrough leadership mentality understand the principle of one more time.

When I am leading a group, my job is to get them to break through barriers. My job is to inspire them and many times if not every time the inspiration is rooted in perseverance. My job is to make them into more than they ever believed they could possibly be on their own. When people break a brick with their fist or a bat with a kick, they develop confidence that they can take on the world. When they win their first sparring match, or even when they survive their first sparring match, they know that they can handle the conflict at work or at school. When they complete a grueling workout, the rest of life looks a little easier.

One of the premises that I have taught for years is, "the more you choose to sweat, the less you have to bleed." While this statement is often applied to sparring, it is relevant for every aspect of life. The more we work to prepare for success in life, the easier success becomes.

Becoming an overnight success in the martial arts world, the business world, or anywhere else, requires years of intense effort.   Monty Hall said, "Actually I'm an overnight success, but it took twenty years."

In the book, Three Feet From Gold, the authors tell a story about how a man gave up everything to mine for gold. At first, the veins were magnificent. The mine looked so promising that the miner sold everything that he had and even got his family and extended family to put in what they could afford. He went back with the equipment, the men, in the belief that he would be rich. The gold ran out very quickly. He dug as long as he could think to dig and eventually he gave up. He sold off the mine and the equipment. The new owner of the mine brought in an expert to give him guidance as to how to make it to the next level in his efforts. The expert, the master, redirected the efforts and the miner dug 3 feet in a new direction. With only 3 feet of digging, he reached the richest gold vein in all of history. The moral of this story is that people often give up when they're only 3 feet from gold.

When you bring in the right leadership to push, inspire, and break through barriers with your teams, you unlock the richest potential that exists. A breakthrough leader will help people keep their eye on the prize and reach their targets. I don't see my life as really any different than anyone else's. There are lots of people in this world the face physical challenges. The difference for me was the attitude that my parents, family and my martial arts instructor helped me to develop in facing the challenges. Because none of us believe in quitting and all of us believe that we can accomplish anything that we want, we break through the challenges and achieve success.

From Jody

Although I have been a martial artist since I was nine years old, my stories of persistence and perseverance relate more to business than anything else. I started a training company in 1999. I did incredibly well for the first two years and sold off that first company.

And Then There Was One

I had started a new company a few months before 9/11 happened. Immediately following that act of terror, training budgets all but disappeared. I was living in Abilene, Texas at the time and there were approximately 6 training companies in that town. With around 120,000 people in the town, we had all the training companies that we needed. My revenues dropped by more than 60% overnight. The next 12 months were grueling. I had to wake up every day and remind myself that this was my calling. I didn't make any money for myself or my family for a year. I did, however, have the opportunity to work 80 hour weeks every week, for free. I made sure that my staff was paid even though I was not. It was during the time that business was the worst that I came up with some of my best ideas. When you face struggles, you begin to think about better ways to do things. I never would've innovated and created new products and services had I not faced that challenge.

Attitude

One of the speeches that I do is on attitude. My favorite part to explain in that speech is the fact that we have a choice in every situation as to what our attitude will be. I use the example of getting a flat tire. If you were driving home and your tire went flat, you would need to pull over and change it. You have two choices to make as you pull the car over. You can choose or be angry and have a flat tire, or you can choose to be happy and have a flat tire. Either way, you have a flat tire.

You have the opportunity to decide what your attitude will be in any and every situation that you face. If you choose an attitude of perseverance, then you will achieve incredible things. Perseverance, like attitude, is a choice. If you choose an attitude that says you will give up when life gets tough, then you will have a very frustrating existence.

When I tested for my brown belt at an Oklahoma TKD school, I broke my fibula on a guys elbow. I had two black eyes and my lips and nose were bleeding. My ribs hurt so bad that it was difficult to breathe. I tested for almost 4 hours, during the summer, in a gym with no air conditioning. I'm thankful that I understood the point of the test. When you get to brown and black, your instructor needs to understand where your heart is. I was exhausted, but I kept coming back. Every time I got knocked down, every time I got bruised, every time I got hit, I remembered the end goal. I went into that test believing absolutely that I would get my brown belt. I had already gotten a black belt in another system. I knew that I could do it. My black belt test was even more grueling than the brown belt test. When you've been able to get back up from five guys hitting and kicking you and come back to break a guy's rib, the rest of life seems pretty tame. More than anything else that I have ever done, martial arts gave me the tools and beliefs to be a success.

What are you doing to help your family be successful later in life? What are you doing to teach perseverance? Do you allow your kids to give up when things get tough? Do you get the demonstration of giving up when things get tough? The TEAM CHIP model doesn't allow people to quit. As a leader, as a breakthrough leader, TEAM CHIP believes that you have to go first. I have seen people's lives transformed by studying under a master. I've seen my own life transformed by studying under a master. Perseverance is a part of who you are and it is developed by overcoming struggles, hardships, obstacles, and all the other stuff that life throws at you.

PERSEVERANCE QUOTES

"Success is a little like wrestling a gorilla. You don't quit when you're tired, you stop when the gorilla is tired." Robert Strauss

"It is easier to move from failure to success than it is from excuses to success." John Maxwell

Lessons From the Masters

Your family is watching you. They're watching to see if you get back up. There watching to see if you will persevere through the tough times and stick things out. Our society has become too disposable. We give up on things too easily. A breakthrough leader knows how to keep going in the face of adversity. They don't quit! They persevere!

You have to make the decision to persevere before you get into the situation that requires it. If you have not decided to persevere, it becomes all too easy to simply make an excuse and quit. If you have decided that you're going to win, no matter what, there isn't anything that anybody can do to persuade you otherwise.

Learning the discipline of martial arts and the practice of perseverance will set your life on a better course than you could imagine. TEAM CHIP doesn't quit. TEAM CHIP won't walk away from the struggle when they are 3 feet from gold. You never really know how close you are to success until you get there. If you believe in the principle of trying one more time, success will become inevitable. It is your perseverance that will get you there.

YOUR BREAKTHROUGH!

You need to remember that you do what you practice. If you "practice" giving up when things get tough, then it is pretty much a guarantee that you will give up when the real world gets tough. The reality that we face is, the real world is tough a LOT.

We want you to remember that if God has allowed a tough time in your life, it's because He knows your heart and knows you can handle it. Every adversity holds within it an opportunity that is equal to or greater than the adversity. The key is to dig in and find that lesson and that opportunity. You must see every challenge as a golden nugget that is hiding beneath the challenge. Finding the positive in the negative will make it easier to gut it out and finish strong. Practice seeing yourself on the other side of this tough time after successfully not giving in or giving up. Draw courage and practice a positive attitude from this vision of your successful self and get busy!!!

A challenge that I will preserver through is...

_____

_____

_____

_____

_____

CHAPTER 11
CONCLUSION

"Affirmation without discipline is the beginning of delusion."
   --Jim Rohn

Becoming a breakthrough leader is a journey that does not end. It is the process of waking up every day and deciding to be the best possible version of yourself that could exist. It isn't about your title, your tenure, or your things. It is about your heart being aligned with the values that make you a positive influence.

Take the time to read and re-read this book. The TEAM CHIP model is not just about martial arts. It is about living the kind of life that you can look back on as a leader and be proud of. It is about living the values that will inspire others to be the highest version of themselves. It is about showing others the pathway to greatness and staying on that journey with them the entire way.

When you absorb this information and spend time focusing on the lessons, you will find that you life will change. The challenge that we have for you is to read this book again over the next two months, focusing on one tenant per week for eight weeks. Live your life that week by the principles that are laid out in that particular chapter. If you are reading about teachable that week, then find ways that you can learn from everyone and everything around you. Truly strive to be teachable in every moment of your life. If you are focused on excellence, ask yourself every morning how you can demonstrate excellence in your work, your relationships, and your life. At the end of the day, write down ways that you have demonstrated excellence.

Get out your highlighter or your pen and write in the margins of the book. Write things that you have observed that relate to the lessons that you have learned. Write out ways in which you are helping others live a breakthrough leadership life. If you will do this, you will see the change happen in your life that leads to the breakthroughs that you desire and deserve. Read through this book at least three times over a six month period, applying the lessons every week. This will help the positive results to become a part of who you are.

Breaking through barriers is a never ending process. There is always one more challenge that we will face. There is always something that presents itself as a barrier to leaving a legacy through our leadership. When you focus on the barrier itself, it can be a real challenge and can often slow you down or even stop you. When you focus beyond the barrier, and remember that you were designed for greatness, then you easily break through to the other side.

Keep your focus on the other side of the barrier, always! Keep your eyes on the prize and keep moving forward. Every challenge that you are presented with is intended to give you the opportunity to grow and become stronger. The reason that we exercise is to break down our muscles and rebuild them even stronger and faster than they were before. The reason that we face challenges as leaders is so we can chip away the things that keep us from being all that we were intended to be and we can break through to success.

Think about how the challenges that you have faced have shaped you. Every challenge presented you with an opportunity for growth. Ask yourself the question… "What can I learn from this challenge?" If you will ask that question with every challenge you face, you will keep learning every single day. Be Teachable!

The final challenge that we have for you is for you to share what you have learned with someone else. Consider the following example…

If we have a dollar and you have a dollar and we exchange them, we are no better off than we were before. We each still have only a dollar. But, if we have an idea and you have an idea and we exchange those, then we are both better off because we now have two ideas each. When you give a copy of this book to friends, family, and business associates, you create a platform for discussing the concepts that have been presented here. We challenge you to help a dozen other people to live a breakthrough leadership life. We challenge you to post the lessons you have learned to share with your friends in social media and use #breakthroughleadership in your posts. We also challenge you to re-read this book several times over the next year to ensure that you truly live a BREAKTHROUGH LEADERSHIP LIFE!

You can purchase copies of <u>Breakthrough Leadership</u> for your friends and family at <u>www.Amazon.com</u>. Give the gift of leadership and growth and help others experience breakthroughs in their lives as well!

RESOURCES

THE BOOKS THAT SHAPED US

I am often asked to share books that I recommend. While I have read literally hundreds of books on Leadership, the following five are significant:

John Maxwell Leadership Bible

Awaken the Giant Within, by Anthony Robbins (This was the first book on leadership that I ever read. It was given to me by a friend who has since passed away. I will forever appreciate the gift. Thank you, Rob.)

7 Habits of Highly Effective People, by Stephen Covey

21 Irrefutable Laws of Leadership, by John C. Maxwell

EntreLeadership, by Dave Ramsey

Think And Grow Rich by Napoleon Hill

The Power of Your Subconscious Mind by Dr. Joseph Murphy

Three Feet From Gold by Sharon Lechter

Leadership Evo by Jody Holland

Teachable *He taught me and said to me, "Let your heart hold fast my words; keep my commandments, and live. Get wisdom; get insight; do not forget, and do not turn away from the words of my mouth. (Proverbs 4:4, 5 ESV)*

Excellence *Finally,*

brothers, whatever is true, whatever is honorable, whatever is just, whatever is pure, whatever is lovely, whatever is commendable, if there is any excellence, if there is anything worthy of praise, think about these things. (Philippians 4:8 ESV)

A *Accountability* Iron sharpens iron, and one man sharpens another. (Proverbs 27:17 ESV)
And no creature is hidden from his sight, but all are naked and exposed to the eyes of him to whom we must give account. (Hebrews 4:13 ESV)

Motivation *But Jesus looked at them and said, "With man this is impossible, but with God all things are possible." (Matthew 19:26 ESV)*

C

Courtesy *And the Lord's servant must not be quarrelsome but kind to everyone, able to teach, patiently enduring evil, (2 Timothy 2:24 ESV)*

Honesty *Better is a poor person who walks in his integrity than one who is crooked in speech and is a fool. (Proverbs 19:1 ESV)*

Inspiration _Show yourself in all respects to be a model of good works, and in your teaching show integrity, dignity, (Titus 2:7 ESV)

P _Perseverance_ But they who

wait for the Lord shall renew their strength; they shall mount up with wings like eagles; they shall run and not be weary; they shall walk and not faint. (Isaiah 40:31 ESV)

ABOUT THE AUTHORS

Chip Townsend is a 6th Degree Black Belt, author, speaker, leader, family-man, and entrepreneur. Chip currently holds 14 World Records for breaking. His speed break of 3 wooden bats set the bar very high for what we are capable of as humans. Chip is married to Glyn Ann, who helps run the Team Chip TKD Centers across Texas and Oklahoma. They have been married for 23 years, and have 3 children; 2 daughters and a son.

Jody Holland is a 2nd Degree Black Belt, author, speaker, and entrepreneur. He focuses on helping individuals and corporations to identify, develop, and retain top performers in their organizations. Jody has been married to Renae for more than 20 years and has two fantastic and fiery daughters. Jody blogs at www.jodynholland.com